“THESE KIDS HAVE CHANGED”

I.S.B.N.: 978-0-8187-0510-6

Hemphill Enterprise

Website Address: education.hemphillent.com

ACKNOWLEDGMENTS

I want to express my gratitude to my family, friends and all the people who've influenced or contributed to my work as an educator, author or consultant.

I'm especially grateful for teachers, administrators, teacher's assistants, students, parents, etc. who continue to provide me with feedback that enhances my work as a consultant in classroom management.

I will always be grateful for the multitude of opportunities I've been given to mentor teachers and conduct classroom management workshops for schools in the metro Detroit area and the state of Ohio. People who've made this possible include but are not limited to Janna Garrison (a former president of the Detroit Federation of Teachers), Bettye Milledge (Senior Regional Director), Dorothy Stanton (retired Detroit Public Schools administrator), Steven & Omega Mostyn (school principals), Paul Gray, Mary Brown & Rose Trotter (retired Detroit Public Schools principals).

I'm also grateful for the opportunities I had to conduct classroom management workshops for The New Teachers Conference (sponsored by the Detroit Federation of Teachers, 1996) and the African American Child In Crisis Conferences held at Cobo Hall (sponsored by Detroit Public Schools Management Academy, 1995 & 1996).

I give personal thanks to former proprietor Allen Wilder for providing a venue where my educational products were available for purchase. (I'm also the author of a set of math cards, Multiplication Facts All By Myself.) Allen owned the Schoolhouse Teachers Store that was located in Detroit, MI.

There are so many people I'd like to name in this acknowledgment, special people who are absolutely dear to my heart and, they know who they are. But I will end this acknowledgment by naming two very special people and a special group of people.

A very special person is Lasenia Jones, a retired principal. Lasenia Jones was my mentor when I was a student teacher. I truly believe I would not be where I am today had it not been for her excellent, strong, caring and supportive guidance during a very crucial time in my life. She would not settle for less than the very best that I had to offer and I am so grateful she didn't.

The most special group of people in my life at this time is my absolutely wonderful and adorable grandchildren, Jada, Mila, Sasha, Taye, Makai and Dakota. It doesn't get any more special than that. I love them dearly and I'm so grateful for them because they continue to motivate me to do what I can to insure kids have the best learning opportunities.

Last, the person who will forever be the most special person in my life, my deceased mother, Mrs. Doris-Hemphill Cherry. I was blessed to have a wonderful mother whose spirit will be with me forever.

CONTENTS

PART II: CLASSROOM MANAGEMENT: MONITORING IN ACTION!

<u>SUPPLEMENT (back of book / unnumbered pages)</u>

Note: In this book, when applicable, the word 'parent' may also represent a legal guardian, grandparent, etc. who has the authority to make decisions on a student's behalf.

INTRODUCTION

THESE KIDS HAVE CHANGED! Yes, many of them have. As I travel through different schools I hear so many teachers, administrators, parents and other adults make this statement. But, guess what, some things haven't changed. First, kids are still *little earthlings* who live on the same planet we do. Second, if we are teaching them, they usually speak the same language we speak, even with all the *language modifications* kids use today. Third, if you earned a Bachelor's Degree or higher to become a teacher, the odds are high that you're older than the kids you teach in elementary, middle and high school. (I'm referring to normal aged kids.) So, kids may have changed but, if you are their teacher, there is something that should never change. *You should always be the adult in charge of the classroom.* You should *expect* students to behave and have a well-written classroom management plan in place to handle situations if they don't. I believed this when I developed and first implemented my classroom management plan in 1984. That belief will never change.

Why did I decide to write a third edition classroom management book? Well, it's a valid question when I consider the fact that I can easily continue using my second edition book, *When Kids Don't Listen*. But, my work as an educator now includes an additional eight years of educational consultant experience. Therefore, the first reason for writing this book is the fact that I have an *I Wish List* of experiences, strategies, etc. that I wish I could have included in my second book.

The second reason for writing this book is based on the fact that many people have asked or suggested that I write a parental version of my classroom management book for parents to use at home. This request has been reinforced by teachers who continue to inform me how much parents appreciate the clarity, simplicity and effectiveness of the plan I developed. So, although this is the first time I've written a version of the plan for parents, I actually accepted a long time ago that I needed to make it happen. But, that acceptance was at a standstill until I recently realized that, not only could I write a parental version, but, I could write one book that could be used by teachers, parents, administrators, churches, other institutions, etc.

That's when I got excited about writing this edition that includes my classroom management plan in its original form but also describes how the plan can be modified for parents and other people to use. This represented a major shift in my thinking because I did not emphasize parental involvement in the first two books I wrote. I also didn't place a great deal of emphasis on administrative involvement either because I believed that teachers needed a classroom management plan that would allow them to literally close classroom doors and teach with minimal help from parents or administrators. I still believe this is the case in many classroom situations. So, although my plan has been revised to include a parental component, etc., teachers who need or desire to implement the original plan will have that option. However, this book will emphasize *new ways to think about old strategies* that will result in creating options for who administrators, teachers, parents, churches, etc. can work with to improve educational opportunities for kids. Strategies will focus on resolving student behavior problems to insure educational goals are accomplished.

I'm excited about the wonderful opportunities teachers, parents and other adults will have if they decide to work together based on information presented in this book. What an awesome opportunity to write a classroom management book that parents can read, utilize and present to schools for consideration of the same. What an awesome opportunity to implement a classroom management plan that has the potential to affect change upon a child's behavior in a home and school. What an awesome opportunity to eliminate the invisible and sometimes tense barrier that too often exists between a parent and a teacher during a parent-teacher conference. That barrier can intensify even more when a parent-teacher conference is requested as a result of inappropriate behavior displayed by a student. I cannot help but be excited about the possibility of contributing to the development of a new relationship between a parent and a teacher that would differ from a traditional one-way relationship in which a parent most often participates as a recipient only of information provided by a teacher.

So now I've written a third edition classroom management book that will not only give teachers opportunities to implement a classroom management plan at school but will also give parents opportunities to implement the plan in homes. YES!! If it hasn't already been done, it's time to do what it takes to bridge the gap between behavioral expectations, strategies, etc. established for students in homes and in schools. No matter what's been said about lack of parental participation in educating kids, if given opportunities, there are parents who are willing to become more involved in doing what it takes to insure teachers have excellent opportunities to educate their children. Also, today more children are being raised by grandparents who need strategies that will help them deal with grandchildren who are more outspoken, etc. than previous generations of children. Therefore I've included a strategy in chapter 5 that can be used by non-custodial parents, grandparents who do not live with grandchildren, etc. who desire to contribute to helping their children, grandchildren, etc. improve efforts to complete assigned tasks in homes.

Once the decision was made to write this book, my desire to find *new ways to think about old strategies* led to an important realization. I realized that a teacher and a parent could work together to implement written student behavior plans. If there is acceptance and agreement between teacher and parent that a student's first classroom is in the home then it's easy to accept that a classroom located in a school is simply an extension of a student's first classroom. Teachers have worked cooperatively for years to insure students are prepared to make the smoothest transition possible from one grade level to the next. A parent and teacher working cooperatively to implement student behavior strategies can narrow or close the gap between behavior strategies implemented for a child at home and at school, thus making it easier for a child to adhere to behavioral expectations in school.

This led to another realization. It's wonderful to talk about parents and teachers working together to implement behavioral strategies that will improve learning environments for students. But, it will probably remain just talk if there are no strategies in place to make it happen. I'm reminded of the 1991-92 school year when I had the opportunity to work as an administrator. During that year there was a great deal of discussion in staff meetings about the implementation of team teaching for the next school year. Several teachers were not excited about the idea. The number one reason was classroom management. They were adamant about not participating in team teaching because they felt student behavior would become even more disruptive than it already was in individual classrooms. I don't think this has changed very much today. However, I believe team teaching is an important strategy but, I believe good classroom management is the foundation for being able to implement it. In this book I will describe several partnerships that can be formed to give people options for who they can work with and how they can work together to resolve student behavior problems.

Reason number three for writing this book results from changes in education that continue to occur as parents have more options for schools their children can attend. This has become a major issue as public charter schools surface throughout the nation. In the past, urban public school systems didn't have to be too concerned with struggling to retain a majority of students. Today, as more and more charter schools open, increasing competition between schools to get and retain students make it even more crucial that schools show they have well-structured and safe learning environments. I believe this situation has also created more opportunities for education consultants who are willing to explore *new ways to think about old strategies* so they can effectively demonstrate new and creative strategies that will help schools improve educational opportunities for students.

A fourth reason that influenced the writing of this book is the major changes that are occurring in teaching staff that provide instruction for students. We now have more people who enter the teaching profession due to making career changes. As a result, reasons for entering the teaching profession have changed and vary greatly from entering simply for the love of teaching and wanting to make a difference in the lives of children. I'm not suggesting that people entering the teaching profession due to changing careers is necessarily negative. But, the bottom line is that some of these people would not have elected to become teachers had they been able to continue in previously held jobs. So again, I believe educational consultants who are willing to do their homework and find *new ways to think about old strategies* can have a major impact as they help people who enter the teaching profession due to career changes. Many of these teachers will bring a wealth of knowledge with them that can help students become more prepared for the real world. Tapping into their experience could possibly change the course of how we educate students, particularly if lower elementary programs were restructured to maximize what some of these teachers can offer. Can we even begin to imagine what it would be like to have a former engineer teaching mathematics at the elementary level, particularly if the engineer team teaches with a certified elementary teacher? As a former math teacher, *I can!* This could be a wonderful and rewarding situation for students as an engineer learns valuable teaching techniques and an elementary teacher gains valuable knowledge for how math concepts apply to the real world. I believe this will be possible if we are willing to find *new ways to think about old strategies*.

A fifth reason for writing this book results from the need to implement strategies that reinforce the behavior of students who display respectful behavior while at the same time insuring that students who display disrespectful behavior are more accountable for thinking before they act. I believe this can be accomplished by implementing several strategies that include giving students opportunities to monitor themselves behaviorally. The ideal reality is that s*tudents should enter schools behaviorally prepared to learn*. But the real reality is that this is unfortunately not the case for too many students. So, what happens for the most part is that we who are in charge, parents, administrators, teachers, etc. implement what I will refer to as *external strategies* to manage student behavior. In other words, we do the majority of the work. Therefore, students are generally *recipients only* of whatever we do. I believe it's time to implement strategies that will give a student opportunities to monitor his/her own behavior so the student can tap into his/her inner-ability to think first before displaying disrespectful behavior. Strategies should also be implemented that reinforce behavior of students who display respectful behavior so they are not tempted to behave differently. Therefore, this book includes strategies on how students can use self-monitoring behavior charts to become active participants in what needs to be done to reinforce good behavior and improve poor behavior.

There are many more reasons I could discuss for writing this book. I've focused on some that I consider most important. Therefore, I believe it's become even more important that I continue expanding my knowledge by using the internet, etc. to find resources, strategies, etc. that will help me continue accomplishing my goals as an educational consultant. This represents a major decision for me at this time in my life because I'm actively involved in music. I'm a jazz vocalist and pianist. But, I now know that my desire to continue making a contribution to improving educational opportunities for students will never end. As long as my health remains good and there are requests for my services or my educational products (multiplication math cards included), I will continue the work that I do. I'm very fortunate to be able to work part-time. Therefore, I have the opportunity to pursue several goals simultaneously.

Again, I'm proud to have written this book that can be used by teachers, parents, administrators, grandparents, parent groups, churches, other institutions or organizations, etc. that desire to become more involved in doing what it takes to improve educational opportunities for kids. If you are a school administrator, teacher, parent, grandparent, guardian, volunteer, representative of an institution or organization, etc. who is willing to join me in accomplishing this goal, this book is for you. Although there will be many references that appear to be directly related to teachers, I recommend that all who are interested in utilizing information presented in this book read it in its entirety. It's important to understand the classroom management system as it was originally developed for teachers because the original plan lays the foundation for all revisions that will be presented in this book. I believe that in this day and time, anyone who wants to make a contribution to improving educational opportunities for students should have a good understanding of what's involved in implementing classroom management plans in schools. I also believe it's important in this day and time that parents and people other than school administrators and teachers implement well-written student behavior plans in non-school environments then consider presenting these plans to schools for consideration to do likewise. A well-written behavior plan that's implemented in a home by a parent, etc. can insure that a child is more receptive to being monitored by a teacher in a classroom. Parents who are willing to implement written behavior plans in homes can also have a major impact on children accepting being monitored by employers later in life.

It is my hope that this book becomes a wonderful resource material that will be used by many people in schools, homes, etc. The following list summarizes some important strategies that will be covered.

- How to use charts to implement a classroom management plan. (Chart examples include a discipline chart for managing student behavior and an individualized assignment chart for advanced students.)

- How teachers, parents, etc. can work individually or together to implement the plan in classrooms and/or in homes.

- How teachers can use documentation sheets for more effective management of individual students who are disruptive in more than one classroom, etc.

- How administrators can use documentation sheets to implement a centralized student behavior plan throughout a school.

- How students can become active participants in monitoring their own behavior.

- How a non-custodial parent, grandparent, etc. can implement a chart to monitor tasks that a child has been assigned to complete in a home.

- How churches and other organizations can work with parents, teachers, etc. to improve learning environments for students.

Today, we can no longer afford to continue a *business as usual* approach for educating kids. We need what I've referred to more than once in this introduction, *new ways to think about old strategies* that result in changes needed to improve learning opportunities for students. It's imperative that parents, teachers, administrators, churches and other organizations, etc. step up efforts to work together to eradicate discipline problems that are occurring in too many schools throughout the nation so that learning opportunities for students can be raised to higher levels.

I appreciate the opportunity to write this book that has already generated a lot of interest. I'm so pleased that I have a track record for having classroom management books in circulation that date back to1994. I'm amazed at what I've accomplished when I consider that my goal in1984 was simply to design and implement a classroom management plan that would allow me to close my door and teach students with minimal help from parents or administrators. I taught in a tough urban school setting where parental involvement was minimal and administrators, no matter how good or kind they were, expected teachers to take care of business and not continually seek administrative help to resolve student behavior problems.

I'm truly grateful for so many people who continue to support me in the work that I do. I'd like to conclude this introduction with the following paragraph.

> It's an awesome experience when administrators, teachers and other school staff persons can work as a team to educate students. It's even more awesome when teachers and parents can work together to improve educational opportunities for students. If we are willing to find new ways to think about old strategies, there are so many more strategies that could be placed in a category of awesome strategies. There's something that happens in the city of Detroit every year that has proven to be a wonderful activity. The activity is, 'Angels Night.' On a yearly basis Detroit citizens come out of their homes and work together to protect homes, businesses and other properties. Now just imagine what the possibilities could be if we applied this strategy to helping schools. In other words, we could name the activity 'Angel's Days' and everyone involved would know when these days were scheduled and would be assigned to schools throughout a city to volunteer their services on designated days. Angel's Night is a well-structured activity that has been successfully implemented in the city of Detroit. An Angel's Days activity could potentially have the same results for schools. I'm asking you to join me in this wonderful adventure as I strive to find new ways to think about old strategies. I wish for all parents, teachers, other adults and organizations great success for all contributions that are made to produce kids who will grow up to become well-educated and productive members of society.

PART I

Classroom Management: Why and How?

Chapter 1 Overview: Do We Really Need Another Classroom Management Book?

- The question is answered based on a goal to get students to assume greater responsibility for displaying respectful behavior in schools. Emphasis is placed on implementing a thorough and well-written classroom management plan that's easy to follow.

Chapter 2 Overview: Don't Blame Me For The Mess!

- The reader is given an opportunity to complete a written survey.
- The roles of a select group of people are discussed for the purpose of examining factors that may affect a person's desire or efforts to do what's necessary to resolve student behavior problems.

Chapter 3 Overview: Lights! Camera! Action!

- The adult in charge must be prepared to manage the behavior of kids. The adult in charge must set the example for kids to follow.

Chapter 4 Overview: Is It The Army, Navy Or Air Force? (Preparing Monitoring Charts)

- This chapter describes how to prepare a set of monitoring charts. Chart examples include a discipline chart, self-monitoring behavior chart, homework chart and other charts to monitor academic and non-academic activities for children in schools and homes.

Chapter 5 Overview: Let's Get Busy! Individual & Partnership Strategies!

- This chapter reinforces information presented in chapter 4. Diagrams are used to display strategies that can be implemented by individuals and people who form partnerships to improve educational opportunities for kids.

1

ally Need Another Classroom Management Book?

e a teacher, administrator, etc. you may very well be thinking that there's enough classroom management books already written that contain good information. But, are you willing to read several books to acquire the information you need? To this day I haven't met many educators who answer yes to this question. For example, teachers usually say they are too busy trying to resolve ongoing student behavior problems to stop and pick up a book that in general doesn't offer long term solutions for these problems. I've always sympathized with teachers who felt this way and, once again, this influenced my decision on how to write this book. So, do we really need another classroom management book? I believe there will always be a need for good classroom management books. But, books written today or in the future should contain classroom management plans that are thorough and easy to follow. They should also place greater emphasis on presenting classroom management plans that make it easier to identify *behavior patterns* of unruly students over short and long periods of time. In other words, greater emphasis should be placed on strategies that make it easier to document this information so students will be less inclined to display unruly behavior.

Let's face facts! For years we've had classroom management books that emphasize what teachers should or shouldn't do. But there are not enough books that emphasize to the same degree what unruly students should or shouldn't do to correct poor student behavior. *Ladies and Gentleman*, I think it's time to stop treating classroom management as if it's a sub-topic of *Alcoholics Anonymous* and therefore, requiring that a teacher go through a *twelve step program* every time he/she attempts to resolve a behavior problem with a disruptive student. I say we're overdue to find *new ways to think about old strategies* that will result in shifting more responsibility onto unruly students to correct unruly behavior, or better still, not display unruly behavior in the first place. For example there's an *old strategy* (if I can call it that) that I consider to this day to be one of the most damaging and counterproductive strategies used by a teacher, administrator, etc. It's presented in the form of a question to a student who has displayed unruly behavior. It may be asked in various ways but, the basic question is, "*Why'd you do it?*" As far as I'm concerned it's an *old question* that at the least, teachers need to delete from strategies used to correct poor student behavior. It's not a bad idea for administrators to consider doing likewise. Asking this question gives a student the opportunity to waste time justifying why he/she displayed unruly behavior. If you've been in education for even a short period of time, you have some understanding of how much instructional time, etc. can be lost as a result of asking this type of question, particularly if it's asked in the presence of a group of students.

I'm going to make a strong statement that clarifies my position on the question. "*There is no acceptable excuse for a student displaying unruly behavior and those of us who are in charge need to stop wasting time giving a student an opportunity to give us an excuse."* It's been my understanding for years that a school counselor or someone in that capacity is the person who should discuss *why* a student displays unruly behavior. Therefore I'm saying, *no counselor or person in that capacity available, no listener!* It's always been that simple for me. During my teaching years I worked as a substitute administrator for one school year. My administrative duties included handling student behavior problems for 7th and 8th graders. This wasn't difficult because students I was in charge of already understood that they would not be given opportunities *after the fact* to waste my time explaining why they displayed unruly behavior in classrooms or other areas of the school. Students quickly developed an understanding of the different between *pre-incident and post-incident* when it came down to whether or not I was interested in listening to any explanations they wanted to give concerning unruly behavior incidents. The work I did that year proved to be a major accomplishment for the entire school because it settled the behavior of students throughout a school that was located in a rough inner-city neighborhood. However, I considered the work I did as an administrator to be an extension of what I was already doing in the classroom. So I was not surprised by the outcome that occurred at that time.

Why do I feel so strongly about not giving students who display unruly behavior opportunities to waste time explaining the behavior? Because, defending the rights of respectful students to have opportunities to learn in positive educational environments has been and will always be a priority for me. I also learned years ago that students who display unruly behavior are inclined to take adults in charge a lot more serious when they realize adults are not interested in giving them opportunities to make excuses for displaying poor behavior.

There has been and continues to be many articles written about the education dilemma for people who are academically unprepared to be hired for available jobs in the workforce. The most recent article I read is dated July 31, 2009 and was printed in a local newspaper. I'm rephrasing an important point discussed in the article and that is, the number of adults who read at or below an acceptable reading level is staggering and number in the thousands. When I read the article I had a flashback to all the years and times that I've seen and continue to see out of control students *running the show* in classrooms. Do we really need to figure out what one of the major problems is in education? There is no doubt in my mind that, among the multitude of adults who can't read, there are thousands and thousands of adults who can't read, not because they didn't try to do the right thing and be respectful students when they were in school, but because they were students in too many classrooms where out of control student behavior consumed instructional time.

Let's examine this problem more thoroughly and *get real* about what happened. If the truth is told, instead of being assigned to classrooms that were suppose to be positive learning environments, in reality, many adults who were respectful students during earlier school years were placed in classrooms that probably felt more like being *sentenced to jail to share cells with unruly cell mates.* Yes! The reality is that unruly students *robbed* themselves and respectful students of opportunities to receive a quality education. Guess what, this continues to be the case in too many schools today.

Now if you think I'm being too harsh, just go and spend some time in a classroom where students display out of control behavior. I assure you, in most cases, five minutes will be more than enough time. Then, while you are there, look around and see if you can find one respectful student who is trying to stay focused on completing assigned class work but appears frustrated as poor behavior is being displayed. Or, what you may see which I think has become more common in recent years is, a student who continues working on assigned work but seems to be taking it all in stride as if it's normal behavior. So now, in either case, you may be observing a student who's not only doing assigned work but, a student who may academically be one of the best students in the group. But, although this student performs well academically, the odds will be high that he/she may be one or more grade levels behind due to being exposed to unruly student behavior for one or more school years. Now, just imagine that, *this is your child in that classroom! Need I say more?*

Therefore, I ask you, is it fair to allow a student who displays unruly behavior to waste time making excuses for the behavior? I think not and I think we've gone way off in left field by continuing to give unruly students more and more opportunities to explain away poor behavior. So you ask, "What is the right question to ask?" (At least this is what I'm hoping if you truly feel you need to even ask a question.) In my opinion, a question that emphasizes student accountability and requires a simple *yes* or *no* response! Students need to *quickly* acknowledge responsibility for displaying poor behavior and do what's needed to correct behavior that should not have occurred in the first place. Examples of what I consider to be better questions are:

- *"Did you have my permission to do what you did?"*
- *"Do you understand that what you did was wrong?"*
- *"Do you believe your actions enhance the learning environment in this classroom?*

It's up to a student to decide how he/she will respond to any question asked. It's preferable that a student respond in a positive manner but, if this doesn't happen, it doesn't change the fact that asking these types of questions makes more sense to me than listening to excuses for poor behavior. After a question has been asked, if necessary, it's important that a student's response is accurately documented for future reference, particularly if the response is negative.

The classroom management plan I developed was designed to document student responses as needed to improve student accountability for correcting poor behavior. As I have already stated, my students understood that lengthy explanations for inappropriate behavior were totally and thoroughly unacceptable to me. Simply put, *I didn't want to hear it because it should never have happened!* I made it clear that I believed a student more often than not had an opportunity to consider how to handle an impending negative situation prior to displaying unruly behavior. Therefore, if necessary, *talk to me first!*

This expectation was included in classroom management strategies I presented to students. On the rare occasions that I gave students opportunities to talk to me, it was understood that instructional time was off limits for discussing student behavior incidents. Students also understood they were given limited opportunities to discuss behavior incidents with me for one purpose only, to insure that problems were resolved for the long term which I defined as *an entire school year* or, better still, *forever*.

I taught school for approximately twenty-five years, from 1976-2001 and I can honestly say that there was only one extreme incident that occurred in my classroom during this time. The incident was a fight that involved two girls. There are people to this day who find it hard to believe that only one fight occurred in my classroom during the fourteen years I taught in middle school. It was quite an interesting situation because students were quietly working on assigned work when, without warning, two girls suddenly jumped up and started fighting. I was later informed that there had been a problem brewing between the girls for several days prior to the incident. Fortunately, my classroom management strategies included instructing students on what to do if a fight occurred. Students were instructed that when I gave the signal, students not involved in the incident should quickly and quietly exit the room and form an orderly line by a set of lockers located across the hall from the classroom. They understood that any student who attempted to *fuel the fight* would be written up as if they were actively involved in the incident. I contacted school security personnel and stood with the class until the girls got tired and stopped fighting. Security reached the classroom about the same time and escorted the girls out of the room. What was most interesting is that both girls took time to apologize to me and straighten the room back up before they were escorted out. They knew I loved to teach and I was fair to all students even though I was *no nonsense* when it came down to managing student behavior.

If it's one thing that we who are in charge of educating students should have learned by now, it's that, if given the opportunity, many unruly students can literally give you a dissertation on why they did something wrong. This opportunity needs to be eliminated but it won't happen if adults in charge fail to pay attention to how and what they say when they interact with unruly students. If this is not done, many questions or comments made by adults in charge will continue to be part of the problems instead of the solutions that are so badly needed to resolve student behavior problems.

I don't think I can say it enough. Classroom management books will be more effective if they present strategies that place greater emphasis on student responsibility for displaying appropriate behavior. Students should be *expected* to enter classrooms *behaviorally prepared* to learn and classroom management strategies should emphasize this. Poor student behavior has escalated to an all time high in classrooms throughout the nation as more and more teachers are at a loss as to what can be done to manage behavior of large groups of students. There are also many parents who continually inform teachers that they want to be supportive but they don't know what to do with their children to correct behavior problems occurring in schools. As I stated before, my classroom management plan has been revised to address parental concerns.

There is one more reason that I revised the plan to include parents that precedes requests from teachers, parents and other people. I will discuss it here because I find it very interesting that it was behavior I displayed as a parent many years ago that was totally the opposite of my behavior as a classroom teacher. The reason dates back to something I realized during the early years of my teaching career but didn't act on at the time. During that time I thought more than once about the fact that the classroom management plan I developed and implemented as a teacher was not directly related to parenting skills I utilized with my children.

I believe it was in the mid-eighties after I had developed and used my classroom management plan for about a year or two before I had the thought that I wished I had consistently applied strategies included in the plan to managing my children's behavior at home. For example, in the classroom I did exactly as I told students I would do. I laid out clearly written guidelines for students to follow, was not repetitive and I systematically used behavior codes to document student behavior. I was very *even keeled* with the way I talked to students and I never yelled in the classroom. That was an accomplish in itself when you consider I spent most of my teaching years teaching a majority of middle school students who were considered to be *tough customers*. There were many years when I was the only teacher who could effectively manage these students behaviorally without yelling or requesting help from parents or administrators.

Well, as I stated, applying the classroom management plan I developed to strategies I used at home was simply wishful thinking and it never happened. *"Didn't I tell you not to…………."* was a common response to something one of my children did that they were asked not to do. Since I'm telling on myself I'll admit I didn't always speak in the quietest voice when I said it either. Would you like to know how many times this statement was repeated? Well…..how high can you count?

Now in school, not only was I rarely if ever repetitive, I implemented a clearly written and easy to understand behavior plan for students to follow. I also utilized responses to inappropriate student behavior that made it clear I expected students to follow the plan I established. These responses shifted responsibility of a student's behavior onto the student. For example, a student would display inappropriate behavior and I'd respond in a very *intelligent* and *calm* manner. (I'm telling the truth here.) The student would then respond by saying something such as, *"I didn't hear you the first time you said it!" or "You only said it one time!"* One of my most common responses to a student's response was (and I'm quoting myself) *"I think one time is enough. Now, if you have a hearing problem that I don't know about, please bring me a note from home to verify the problem."* I usually added a comment about the student following up with verification from a doctor, etc. I can tell you that I had a wonderful time interacting with my students and many times found myself trying to maintain professional composure and not smile or laugh when I responded with comments such as the one just stated. To this day, I believe my ability to incorporate subtle humor from time to time into comments I made to students who violated rules contributed to my being able to form a loving bond with the majority of my students, including disruptive students. However, getting back to the point

I'm trying to make, the bottom line was that my students knew I meant business about not being repetitive.

Now, what was this plan that worked so well in school but was not implemented with my children? My plan, *The Classroom Monitoring System*, was based on using a set of charts to manage student activities and included a chart that was developed exclusively to manage student behavior. I developed the plan in 1984 which was the first year in my teaching career that I went from teaching small groups of students in a math lab to teaching large classes of thirty-five or more students. In the math lab I used charts to track multiple math skills for students in grades 5-8. I quickly realized after being assigned to a classroom to teach 7th and 8th grade mathematics that I could apply a *charting approach* to managing student behavior and other student activities. An example of other student activities that were eventually included in the classroom monitoring system were individualized assignments for advanced students, a math game activity for all students, random activities such as sending a class syllabus or other handouts home, etc.

The discipline chart was crucial to implementation of my classroom management plan. This chart laid the foundation for being able to use a set of charts to manage several student activities. The discipline chart clearly established each student's behavior pattern over a long period of time. Peer pressure was a major component that made the chart a successful tool for managing student behavior. Students had tremendous interest in how their behavior patterns could be compared to each other and this interest continues today as I get feedback from teachers who are using the plan. As my plan expanded to include monitoring several student activities, I began to realize the value of becoming more of a facilitator and less of a lecturer.

I will clarify again that the original purpose for developing the plan in 1984 was to simply be able to close the door to my classroom, effectively manage student behavior and teach. (I'm just keeping it real.) Yes! I never intended to promote the plan by becoming an educational consultant who would do workshops, work with other teachers, etc. I simply wanted to manage student behavior with little or no assistance from administrators and/or parents. I considered it to be less stressful and more productive to work directly with students by implementing a well-written monitoring system that students could understand and follow.

When did my educational consultant work begin? My consultant work actually began when co-workers observed and commented on how well students behaved and worked in my classroom. This led to me helping a veteran teacher who'd struggled unsuccessfully for years to manage disruptive students. The teacher soon had a classroom where students behaved appropriately and worked cooperatively. Other co-workers soon started requesting my help but it became impossible for me to continue giving up preparation periods to accommodate requests. After several years of being asked to write a classroom management book I responded by writing the first book in 1994.

Why did the classroom monitoring system prove effective? There were many reasons. The system minimized dependency on parental and administrative support. Students' desire to maintain good behavior improved when poor behavior was consistently documented on a discipline chart that contained names of an entire class. A discipline chart clearly displayed behavior patterns of disruptive students. People reading the chart had an opportunity to rank the degree of disruptive behavior for applicable students. Administrators, parents and students were given an opportunity to see the chart. It was a win-win situation that resulted in classrooms where teachers had more opportunity to teach because less time was spent on discipline. Once I implemented the classroom monitoring system, I was absolutely committed to implementing it every day I taught school until the day I retired in 2001.

My consultant work today includes mentoring a teacher who was one of my middle school math students during the 1980's. This teacher's classroom is patterned after mine and she informed me that she implemented classroom management strategies based on what she learned from me during the years she was one of my students. I'm so proud of this young lady and I will say that if I was assigned to more teachers like her I'd probably be out of work before too long. The only reason I was asked to look in on this teacher was because she was in her first year of teaching in a school I consulted for and it was standard procedure for the principal to assign teachers new to the school to be observed and mentored by a consultant. It was tremendously rewarding for me to encounter this teacher and I'd love for this to happen more often as I continue my work.

Why do I believe charts are an effective tool for managing student activities? Charts provide a systematic and fair method for displaying a great deal of information for a group of students. Again, a discipline chart can display student behavior patterns over a long period of time. Therefore, a student is given opportunities to clearly see how his/her behavior pattern relates to behavior patterns of peers. I don't believe students should have to wait until they become adults to work for a company or go into the armed services to experience what it's like to be *behaviorally monitored* in writing. If students are given this experience early in life, particularly if it starts with parents in homes, it will better prepare them for being monitored, evaluated, etc. as students in schools, adults working for companies, etc. Just imagine the time teachers wouldn't waste in classrooms if kids came to school with this type of experience under their belt. Using charts to monitor student behavior can also enhance a teacher's opportunities to develop classroom activities that will allow a teacher to facilitate more and lecture less. The more teachers become facilitators the greater the opportunities to affect changes that will improve educational opportunities for students. However, the reality is, implementing a written monitoring procedure to manage student behavior is not a natural process for many children. As a result, there are too many children who unfortunately will not hesitate to let classroom teachers know they disapprove of a procedure that's implemented to systematically monitor their behavior in writing. Therefore, it's critical that parents consider implementing this type of procedure in homes in an effort to eliminate or minimize stress some children experience if they are exposed to this procedure for the first time in schools.

The classroom management plan in this book also includes revisions that describe strategies parents and teachers can implement by forming partnerships. These partnerships can result in better management of student behavior in schools and in homes. Using charts to manage student behavior can have several benefits for teachers and parents that include not being verbally repetitive and not having to memorize detailed information that needs to be referenced at a later time or date.

Now, back to the original question, do we really need another classroom management book? I say yes, we can always use another book. Existing books offer a wealth of strategies, suggestions and ideas that have and will continue to help teachers. But, I will suggest that much of what's written in existing books can be defined as *band aid solutions* for extremely destructive and long term student behavior problems that have only gotten worse in schools throughout the nation. So we continue to get what I refer to as a lot of short term classroom management strategies that don't do very much to improve extremely poor student behavior over the long term.

For example, many teachers have been told for years that wonderful lesson plans can improve student behavior. Well, I don't disagree. They can. But I hate to think that I could never again ask a student to simply open a book, turn to an assigned page and complete assigned problems on that page without me trying to figure out how to perform like I'm in a play to get the student to open the book. I will concede that a teacher should not be one dimensional in how he/she present lessons. A teacher should be excited about teaching but students must also be excited about learning and displaying respectful behavior so a teacher has great opportunities to teach.

There's one word that pretty well summarizes what the basis of a relationship between teacher and student must be if a student has any hope of receiving a quality education. In 2008 I was given the opportunity to discuss my feelings about this word during an interview for a cable TV program. The word is, RESPECT! If you look the word up in a dictionary, you'll find that the definition of the word *respect* is the same today as it was when I started teaching in 1976. '*Respect means to show consideration for something or someone.*' The meaning of the word has not been watered down in dictionaries and it shouldn't be watered down by allowing students to dance around the fact that this is what they need to do to receive a quality education. The fact of the matter is, for too many students, if we who are in charge don't *expect* them to behave, we can *expect* them to show *disrespect* for the learning process!

Therefore I will continue to believe that we need more classroom management books that don't ignore or minimize student responsibility for displaying appropriate behavior. This book continues my commitment to offer strategies that will improve educational environments for kids everywhere. I've also taken to heart suggestions, requests, etc. that I write a book that gives readers, workshop participants, etc. opportunities to write information in the book as it's being read. I appreciate the opportunity to write this book in such a way that teachers, parents, etc. have the opportunity to write responses in the book and follow up with discussions, etc.

There's one more very important thing that I want to discuss in more detail, the role that churches can play to resolve this ongoing crisis. I have believed for many years that churches are one of the most powerful institutions that can make a difference in improving educational opportunities for kids. It's definitely time for *new ways to think about old strategies*, time for new and strategic partnerships to be formed between schools and churches. But I will say on behalf of churches, other institutions and organizations that they should not be expected to become involved with schools that are not making a good effort and showing success with managing student behavior. They should also not be expected to become involved with schools that don't have well structured and detailed plans in place for how churches, etc. can contribute to helping schools.

So here we are, at a time in history where, in education, we have truly reached the fork in the road. As a nation, we must decide, do we continue down the road where little or no changes will be made to implement better classroom management strategies that will result in improved educational opportunities for students or do we take the road that will give us opportunities to join forces and make needed changes? It is definitely time to find *new ways to think about old strategies*. Those of us who truly believe that *it takes a village to raise a child* need to put the meaning of this phrase into action and get serious about applying it to educating students. We cannot continue functioning off of an individualistic or self-centered mentality that prevents us from doing everything possible to work as if we are team-players on one big team whose goal is to provide quality education for *all students who are willing to respect learning environments*. Classroom management books must be continuously updated so that we as a nation can accomplish desired educational goals. These books must contain updated strategies for those of us who are willing to respond to the following statement.

"Do not just ask

what SCHOOLS can do to improve learning environments for kids,

but ask

what YOU can do to improve learning environments for kids!"

2

Don't Blame Me For The Mess!

The title of this book, *These Kids Have Changed*, summarizes why so many people say *no thanks* to entering or continuing in the teaching profession. It is also one of the reasons why many people outside the teaching profession choose not to volunteer their time or make financial contributions to help schools. Because, as much as we may want to believe those four words imply positive change when spoken, that's generally not the case. The phrase, *these kids have changed*, is a major factor for ongoing discussions and no shortage of laundry lists for who should assume responsibility for correcting poor student behavior that has spiraled so far out of control and goes unchecked in too many schools. If you ask an administrator, teacher, parent, representative of an organization, etc. to write a list of reasons for the dilemma, you'll probably get several different lists that will vary depending on how much the writer is willing to assume responsibility for helping to resolve the dilemma. The following survey has been prepared to give you an opportunity to respond to questions concerning this issue. This survey can also be completed by a representative of a church, organization, etc.

•Role Survey•

Please circle the word that best defines your role or fill in the blank space.

Parent Teacher Administrator Other: ____________________________________

Answer or circle your choice for each question.

1. Who do you believe should assume number one responsibility for correcting poor student behavior?

   Administrator Teacher Student Parent Other: ______________

2. Why do you believe the person, institution, etc. that you selected in the previous question should assume number one responsibility for correcting poor student behavior?

   ____
   ____
   ____
   ____

3. List two strategies that you believe the person, institution, etc. selected in number one can use to help correct poor student behavior.

a. ______________________________

b. ______________________________

4. Do strategies you listed for number 3 take into consideration how respectful students are affected by poor student behavior? Explain.

5. If you could change roles with the person, institution, etc. you selected in number one and had time to really think about the responsibilities attached to that role, do you think your answer for number one would be different? Answer *yes* or *no* and explain.

6. Are you willing to participate in a partnership to implement strategies that will help correct poor student behavior and/or improve educational opportunities for students? (Example of partnerships: teacher & parent, church & school) Circle _yes_ or _no._ If you circle yes, give two examples for what you are willing to do. If you circle no, please explain why.

Yes No

a. ______________________________

b. ______________________________

7. Discuss or list suggestions for how your answers for questions 1-6 can be used to improve student behavior.

Now that you've had an opportunity to complete the *role survey*, I'd like to discuss roles of a select group of people and institutions. This select group of people and institutions do not represent all people or institutions that can contribute to efforts that are made to improve educational opportunities for kids. However, they represent some that I believe are most important. This discussion will hopefully bring to the forefront thoughts, attitudes, behaviors, etc. that may prevent a person or institution from developing a mindset that is needed to enhance or create opportunities to work with others to resolve student behavior problems. This chapter also includes three fictional skits that I wrote. Two of the skits are representative of interactions that occurred many times between teachers and students during the years I taught school. The titles of these skits are *'Please'* and *'Let.'* The third skit is more reflective of *a stretch of the imagination* when I think about the many *enjoyable* discussions I had years ago with co-workers concerning the kinds of strategies one might use to get an unwilling parent to come into a school to resolve a problem with an unruly student. The title of the skit is *'Everything.'* Although classroom management is a serious issue, everything that happens during interactions pertaining to this issue is not always as serious. There are many experiences with unruly students that are resolved when spontaneous and/or humorous comments are interjected into verbal exchanges between teacher and students. I'm fairly certain these skits will bring back memories for some of you who've taught or interacted with students for any length of time. Skits may also be a wonderful way to start a classroom management session if there are good actors available. There's usually a wealth of talent among staff persons.

Before discussing roles of a select group of people I'd like to reprint a poem I wrote and included in a classroom management article dated April 2006. The title of the article and poem is, *Order In The Court!* I've always believed that a classroom is a teacher's courtroom and is therefore just as important as a courtroom where sessions are conducted by a judge. Courtroom participants have no option but to behave or face the possibility of immediate expulsion from the premises. The same should be true for students who refuse to display respectful behavior in classrooms.

ORDER IN THE COURT!!

YOU'RE IN THE CLASSROOM NOW!
YOU CANNOT WALK THE FLOOR!
DIRECTIONS GIVEN THAT WILL BE FOLLOWED
OR YOU MUST EXIT THE DOOR!

FOR LOUD I WILL NOT BE!
I'LL USE MY EYES TO SEE!
YOU RAISE YOUR HAND TO SPEAK
OR OUT YOU'LL GO THIS WEEK!

NO NONSENSE IN HERE TODAY!
RESPECT IS THE ONLY WAY
OR I'LL HAVE ONE THING TO SAY!
YOU CAN'T COME BACK TODAY!

• Role 1: The Teacher •

Skit: "PLEASE!"

Characters: Teacher / Ms. Johnson   Disruptive student / Jay   Several other students

Setting

Ms. Johnson is writing an assignment on a board as several students talk loudly without permission. She abruptly stops writing and turns towards the class just in time to see balled up paper thrown across the room. Although Jay is surrounded by several students, she's sure he threw the paper. She's upset as she glares at the class. Students quiet down as she angrily talks to the group.

Scene

Ms. Johnson
I can't even turn my back for one minute to write work on the board without you acting like I'm not even in the room! It just doesn't make sense! Now, would you *PLEEEASE* answer one question for me! I just want to know, how many of you went to church last Sunday??

(Several students, including students who displayed out of control behavior, slowly raise their hands.)

Ms. Johnson
That's what I thought! Now, if the preacher didn't have to tell you to be quiet when he…or she was *PREACHING, PLEEEASE* tell me why I have to tell you to be quiet when I'm *TEACHING!!*

(Several students look embarrassed but no one responds to the question.)

Ms. Johnson
…and Jay, if I have to tell you *One More Time* to stop throwing paper, I'm going to *Lose My Mind!*

Jay
I didn't do it!

Ms. Johnson
Oh *PLEEEASE*!!! Jay, I know it was you who threw that piece of paper!

Jay
Prove it!

(*Ms. Johnson pauses for several seconds as 35 pairs of eyes stare at her. She knows they're waiting to see what her next move will be. She's extremely upset as she stares at the class. She does not speak out loud as she slowly and continuously starts moving her head from left to right. Her lips are tight as she thinks the following.*)

Ms. Johnson
I got to pray! *RIGHT HERE and RIGHT NOW! PLEEEASE* just let me make it to June of next year and *PLEEEESE* don't let the number to the retirement office be busy when I call and *PLEEEASE* don't let my retirement papers get lost in the mail!!

(Ms. Johnson stops shaking her head but is still upset as she speaks to the class.)

"Will you PLEEEASE…. do me a favor and act like I'm preaching instead of teaching!!"

Now I'll be the first to admit this is not the most desirable way to handle a disruptive situation with a group of students. But it is characteristic of what happens in some classrooms when teachers are upset and fed up with disruptive student behavior. If you are a classroom teacher you certainly don't want to start out or end up in a similar predicament. But the fact of the matter is that you may have students who will display unruly behavior an entire school year if it goes unchecked. If you are like many teachers, you don't have the option to retire in the immediate future. Even if you do, one day can seem like an eternity if you are dealing with unruly students the entire day. So, what are your options? Well, if you don't implement a well-written classroom management plan, you can spend an entire school year being *reactive,* you know, doing things like yelling, begging unruly students to behave, etc. I don't think that will be much fun and it could result in increased visits to a doctor's office. I've worked with several teachers that this happened to. The majority of them eventually reached the point where they accepted that implementing a well-written classroom management plan was a better option. That's when several co-workers sought my help years ago. Today, constant changes in education have resulted in a growing number of teachers not knowing from year to year where they will teach. This uncertainty makes it even more important that you are prepared to implement a well-written classroom management plan no matter where you end up at. It's better to be prepared to implement a plan and not need to use it than to need it and not have one prepared for use.

If you decide to implement a well-written classroom management plan you basically have two options. You can implement a plan by yourself or work with other adults to implement it. As I have already stated, the plan presented in this book still includes the original plan I developed and can be used by a teacher who decides to work by him/her self to implement the plan. However, in this day and time, I encourage you to make the effort to form partnerships with co-workers, parents, etc. This can lessen the burden of working alone to resolve student behavior problems and help close loopholes unruly students have jumped through for years as they play adults in charge against each other.

Therefore, if there's a parent group in your school, I believe it would be wise to consider working with the group. This could make it easier to organize supportive parents throughout the school who are willing to work with school staff persons to resolve student behavior problems. I also suggest that you consider working with a committee of teachers, parents, administrators, etc. to develop and implement a school wide student behavior plan that clearly explains how volunteers, monetary contributions, etc. can or will be used. Churches and other organizations may be more inclined to send volunteers into schools that are organized, well run and can demonstrate that a plan is in place for effective use of volunteers, monetary donations, etc.

The time has definitely arrived when, at the least, teachers should be willing to form partnerships with supportive parents for the purpose of resolving student behavior problems. If there is acceptance and agreement between teacher and parent that a student's first classroom is in the home, this could enhance efforts to work together to implement a plan that connects behavior strategies used in a home to behavior strategies used in a school. This could potentially make it easier for a student to follow a classroom management plan that's implemented in a school. A parent-teacher partnership can also empower parents to work with teachers in such a way that parents become more than just people who are on the receiving end of information given during parent-teacher conferences. It's a reasonable decision to include parents in implementation of classroom management strategies because parents generally spend more time with their kids than teachers do. Therefore, a parent has more time to implement behavior management strategies in the home and most certainly has a greater opportunity to impact changes in a child's behavior.

There are many parents who are supportive of teachers. These parents include parents who readily admit they don't know what to do to resolve behavior problems their children have in schools. I believe some of these parents will be more than appreciative of a plan that gives them opportunities to work with teachers to resolve student behavior problems. Therefore, I'm saying that it is definitely time to be proactive and create more opportunities for parents and teachers to form partnerships to address student behavior problems. If you are a teacher who's willing to form this type of partnership with parents, you just may reap the benefit of the word 'retirement' being foreign to your vocabulary for many years to come.

• Role 2: The Parent •

"I send my child to school to learn. I expect the teacher to teach everything my child should know by the end of the school year!"

I think it's called, *great expectation!* If you are a parent who has a well-behaved child, it's reasonable that you expect your child to respect the learning process and successfully master a minimum of one grade level of education for each school year. It's also foreseeable that you will have wonderful interactions with your child's teacher/s. However, the odds are high that you will continue to experience a traditional relationship with a teacher where you are on the receiving end of getting information about your child's progress in school. This type of relationship usually works as long as your child attends a school where children have wonderful and uninterrupted opportunities to learn as a result of not being distracted by unruly student behavior. But, if the opposite is true, are you willing to form partnerships with teachers who are willing to work with you to do what it takes to help maintain environments your child and other children can learn in? This does not necessarily mean you have to physically work in a classroom with a teacher. In fact, the plan presented in this book will give you an opportunity to implement classroom management strategies in your home and encourage other parents to do likewise.

There are ongoing discussions and articles written about lack of parental support in schools. I believe it's important that you understand that lack of parental support can be the result of parents of respectful students not doing anything to help teachers as well as parents of disrespectful students who refuse to support teachers. So much is happening in schools today that I believe it's critical that you see beyond what's happening with your respectful child or children and do what it takes to help as many teachers as you can in a school or schools your child or children attend. If applicable, at the least, it's critical that you participate in or help form a strong parent group that will support organized efforts of teachers to implement plans for the purpose of resolving student behavior problems.

If you are a parent of a child whose behavior is not good in school, if applicable, it's even more important that you accept the fact that your child's behavior is causing your child and other children to lose instructional time. It's critical that you don't adopt a defensive attitude that prevents you from being supportive of teachers. A non-supportive or defensive attitude could result in your child eventually becoming part of a growing number of adults who are not educationally prepared to qualify for good jobs. If applicable, it's important that you make a commitment to do what it takes to resolve behavior problems or, at the least, accept that your child can't be allowed to expose other children to negative behavior. Just imagine that, if the majority of parents of children who display inappropriate behavior accepted the responsibility of making positive contributions to resolve student behavior problems, learning environments in a majority of schools would show immediate improvement that would be felt throughout the nation. Although this may never be the case, if applicable, you certainly have an opportunity to make the decision to take your name off *the unsupportive parents' list*.

It is definitely time for parents to do more than just be on the receiving end of information about their children's progress in schools. It's time for parent-teacher partnerships to be formed that will result in parents implementing components of well-written classroom management plans in homes so children will consider it a natural process to follow well-written classroom management plans that are implemented in schools.

Partnerships between parents and teachers can also be strengthened by parent groups that work with schools to implement strategies to resolve student behavior problems. As a parent, your participation in a parent group is critical, greatly needed and can strengthen your position as a parent who can make a difference. A positive and successful effort on your part can reinforce the efforts of teachers, administrators, etc. to create positive learning environments for all students who are willing to respect the learning process. It would be wonderful for you to be able to say the following:

"There's no doubt in my mind that my child is receiving a quality education because I've formed partnerships with teachers to make it happen for all children who show respect for the learning process."

•Role 3: The School Administrator •

Skit: "EVERYTHING!"

Characters: School Principal / Mr. Johns Teacher / Ms. Johnson Narrator

Setting

Ms. Johnson is upset as she talks with Mr. Johns about Jay's repetitive poor behavior. She's written several behavior referrals and now wants Mr. Johns to give Jay a 5 day suspension from school.

Scene

Ms. Johnson
Mr. Johns, I've done *EVERYTHING* I can to get Jay to act better!

Mr. Johns
EVERYTHING??

Ms. Johnson
Yes!! *EVERYTHING!*

Mr. Johns
Okay! Give me three examples of what you've done!

Ms. Johnson
Okay! I CAN DO THAT! I've tried several times to reach Jay's mother by telephone. So, *EXAMPLE NUMBER 1*, the first time I called the number Jay gave me, I was told I had the wrong number! *EXAMPLE NUMBER 2*, the second time I called the number Jay gave me, I was told it was no longer in service! Then, Jay gave me another number to call and had the nerve to say, he hoped this one would work! So, *EXAMPLE NUMBER 3*, I called that number and the person who answered the phone angrily told me that she was tired of people calling her number to speak to Jay's parents. She had no idea who he was!

(*Ms. Johnson pauses*)

Mr. Johns
Is that *EVERYTHING?*

Ms. Johnson (*look increasingly agitated*)
Yes Mr. Johns! That's *EVERYTHING!* Now will you pleeeeease suspend Jay for at least five days so the other students can get a break from being exposed to his nonsense? You do agree with *EVERYTHING* I wrote in his referrals that I sent to you?

Mr. Johns
I concur!

Ms. Johnson
Absolutely?? With *EVERYTHING??*

skit continued from previous page

Mr. Johns
Yes, *EVERYTHING!* BUT....we must contact Jay's mother first before I can suspend him, or my hands are tied.

Ms. Johnson
Is that *EVERYTHING* you can do?

Mr. Johns
Yes Ms. Johnson! That's *EVERYTHING!*

Ms. Johnson (*has a mischievous look on her face*)
Mr. Johns, if I can come up with a plan to get Jay's mom up here, can you have a 5 day suspension letter ready to give her.

Mr. Johns
I can do that!

Ms. Johnson
Thank you Mr. Johns! I will have a plan ready for your approval by the end of the day! If it meets with your approval, *EVERYTHING* will be taken care of in a few days!

(*Ms. Johnson smiles as she walks away from Mr. Johns.*)

Narrator
Four days later a limo pulls up to the school. Jay's mother is sharply dressed as the limo driver holds the door for her to exit the limo. She exits the limo and proudly walks into the school to meet with Mr. Johns who's been informed of her arrival. Ms. Johnson had contacted Jay's mother by mail and informed her she was being treated to lunch at a fancy restaurant. The purpose would be a surprise that Mr. Johns would give her when the limo driver brought her by the school before taking her back home after lunch at the fancy restaurant. Of course Jay's mom assumed this was all for a good purpose and therefore accepted the invitation. When Jay's mom entered the school she saw Mr. Johns who was standing near the main office. When she reached Mr. Johns, she extended her right hand to shake his right hand. Mr. Johns quickly shook her hand then just as quickly used his left hand to hand her an envelope that contained Jay's suspension letter. The envelope also contained an explanation for what happened with the attempts Ms. Johnson made to call Jay's home. Mr. Johns proceeded to tell Jay's mom that it was good meeting her and he hoped she had plans to attend the next scheduled parent-teacher conference. He then told her to have a good day but, he clarified that there was no more money in the school's budget to treat her to another lunch or send a limo driver to pick her up for the conference!

Although this skit doesn't represent any real life situation that I'm aware of, it does represent some of the *humorous* thoughts I've had about how situations with uncooperative parents could be handled. I can also say that the majority of administrators I've worked with have been wonderful and I've shared many *interesting* conversations with them about how to resolve problems with uncooperative parents. Even if they were not willing to foot the bill to send a limo driver to pick up an uncooperative parent, they were willing to do whatever they could within reason to provide the leadership and support that was needed to insure students had a safe and positive learning environment. To do otherwise usually results in low morale among school staff persons. Low morale makes it difficult as a school year progresses to consistently and effectively implement strategies to resolve student behavior problems. It's unfortunate that some school administrators do not consistently sustain efforts to effectively manage student behavior throughout schools they are in charge of. Reasons for this ongoing dilemma increase as parents are given more options for schools they can enroll their children in.

Today many school administrators struggle more and more to maintain desired student enrollments. This has resulted in an increase of disruptive students that are not held accountable for their behavior because school administrators are reluctant to suspend students from classrooms and/or schools. There are an increasing number of parents who will not hesitate to transfer their children to more than one school within a school year if they become unhappy with schools their children attend. Unfortunately, for some parents, it doesn't matter if reasons for transfers are justifiable or not. The options for schools children can attend continue to increase and many parents will simply make the choice to move their children. The dilemma for school administrators only gets worse as disruptive students take advantage of the situation knowing that there is reluctance on the part of school administrators to suspend them from schools.

So, if you are an administrator who's faced with this dilemma, is there something you can do to address the problem? Can you afford not to find *new ways to think about old strategies* that will help resolve this growing dilemma? It's crucial that the problem is resolved because it is absolutely unfair for respectful students to be deprived of quality educational opportunities as a result of students who refuse to respect the learning process. I believe there are solutions for this dilemma but solutions must emphasize school wide student behavior plans that are consistently implemented by school staffs that operate as cohesive teams. These plans must also include components that will give students opportunities to participate in self-monitoring procedures. A student who insists upon displaying *unruly* behavior should be responsible for documenting his/her own behavior at the point the behavior occurs. The addition of a self-monitoring component for students is possibly the most important component that's missing from many school wide student behavior plans. This component can serve to decrease opportunities for students to act as if they are not aware of unruly behavior at the point the behavior is displayed. The goal of a self-monitoring procedure is to give students the opportunity to think before displaying inappropriate behavior that they will be required to document on self-monitoring charts. This strategy can help students develop the inner discipline that's so often missing when their behavior is documented, monitored, etc. by people other than themselves. A school wide plan should also include strategies that give supportive parents opportunities to participate in implementation of strategies to improve student behavior.

Therefore, as a school administrator, if applicable, it's critical that you are willing to take your role as a team leader to another level to insure students understand administrators, teachers, supportive parents, etc. are working as one big team to implement a plan that will produce desired results for improving student behavior throughout a school. For example, administrators generally place tremendous emphasis on teachers assigning homework for students. The plan that's presented in this book will now take self-monitoring of student behavior and completion of homework assignments to another level by including specialized charts for these activities. This will be demonstrated in chapter 4.

As an administrator it's also important that a school wide student behavior plan include effective strategies for how non-teaching school staff persons can be used to participate in implementation of a school wide student behavior plan. Chapter 5 will include strategies for effective utilization of non-teaching staff persons, outside volunteers, institutions, etc. It is of utmost importance that a school administrator is willing and able to speak on behalf of a school by saying:

"One of the goals of our school is for school staff to work more cohesively as a team to help students become more self-disciplined so that we can decrease the amount of time we spend resolving student behavior problems and increase the amount of time students spend on academic activities."

• Role 4: Churches •

Church Representative-Statements:

- *"Our church has a charter school. This is our contribution to educating students."*
- *"Our church gives charitable donations to lots of organizations and needy people. We prepare food baskets for the poor for special holidays like Thanksgiving and Christmas."*

"Let the people say, AMEN!" First, I'd like to say that I commend those churches that are making positive contributions to communities and to educating students. If *every church* made contributions to educating students such as establishing a well-run charter school, sending volunteers into schools, donating money to schools for educational resources, etc. it could change the course of what's happening in education forever. Therefore, if your church has established a charter school, that's wonderful and most certainly represents a positive contribution towards educating kids.

The only question I believe your church then needs to ask is, "Can more contributions be made and, if so, what will they be?" Well, let's take time and consider the following example for a church that has opened a charter school. There's possibly more than one teacher, administrator and/or other school staff person in your church congregation who doesn't teach in the charter school established by your church. Also, there are possibly children in your congregation who attend other schools. Therefore, what about those children and/or children in other schools? Do they deserve less opportunity to benefit from help your church can provide simply because they don't attend a charter school that's been established by your church?

There is one very obvious and important fact about churches that I believe can make a major difference in the support churches can provide. There are a *trillion* more churches than schools. Well, maybe I'm stretching it a little but, the ratio of churches to schools in many areas of the nation are such that it's foreseeable that every school has the potential to be adopted by three or more churches that can contribute volunteer support, monetary contributions, etc. to that school alone. There's a humorous question that I hear often and that question is, *"Am I preaching to the choir?"*

What I'm suggesting is that, if applicable, a church be willing to *mentally* remove the walls that enclose it and work with other churches (two or more) to help one school. For example, one church could initiate this strategy by contacting other churches to request that a team of churches work together to help one or more schools. Each church involved could then select one or more representatives who will meet together to discuss strategies, ideas, etc. that can be presented to a school principal or school leader. Strategies can then be discussed and finalized for how a team of churches will help a school.

Schools can also select representatives to contact churches to request support. A school representative may have even more credibility if he/she is a member of a church that is contacted. A school representative should be able to present or verify that a school wide plan is in place to validate a request being made to a church.

The help that churches are willing to provide should be very specific. For example, one church may contribute to helping math teachers only while another church may contribute to helping first grade teachers only. A church should verify that a school has a well-written plan for how a church's donations, volunteers, etc. will be used. A church should also verify that a school's plan include an evaluative component to follow up the effectiveness of contributions made by a church.

I applaud churches that are making a difference for students but I will continue to believe that there are so many more churches that can make a difference such that the following statement could apply to a majority of churches.

"We have the power to do what it takes to insure that every student in America who wants a quality education will get one."

• Role 5: Other Institutions, Organizations, Etc. •

CEO of an Organization, Company, etc.:

"I cannot afford to give my employees regularly scheduled time off from work to work as volunteers in schools."

There is much that other institutions, organizations, companies, etc. can do to find *new ways to think about old strategies* that will help resolve student behavior issues. Academic lessons that involve real life experiences are usually more interesting for students, including students who have a habit of displaying unruly behavior. Many institutions, organization, etc. already send professional representatives into schools for Career Day activities, etc. I'm now suggesting that some of these professionals such as engineers, nurses, etc. be given opportunities to work with schools on a more regular basis to insure lessons are relevant to real life experiences and more interesting for students. As I stated before, we cannot afford to continue business as usual when it comes to educating students. I recently read in the newspaper that a firm is giving employees the opportunity to volunteer up to 10 hours of scheduled work time a month to help other organizations. Students need more real life examples for work opportunities that will be available to them if they are successful in their academic studies. Just imagine the difference it would make if every company did what this one company is doing. If you are the owner, head executive, etc. of a company, etc., if applicable, it is hoped that you will soon say:

"I cannot afford NOT to give my employees regularly scheduled time off from work to work as volunteers in schools."

This chapter would not be complete without a discussion of the roles of a respectful and disrespectful student. It's crucial that we clearly understand each student's role from the point of view of the student to insure we do what's needed to *protect the rights of respectful students and correct the behavior of disrespectful students*.

•Role 6: The Respectful Student •

"I want to learn in Mrs. Wright's class but the kids won't listen to her. They play and yell in her room everyday."

Ah yes! How refreshing it is to have respectful students in a classroom but how sad it is to hear a respectful student say the opening statement for this discussion. Respectful students may represent a minority in many classrooms but, they still exist and they deserve the best that parents, teachers, administrators, etc. have to offer. Those of us who are in charge must be willing to do what it takes so respectful students don't continue falling farther and farther behind in reaching educational goals due to unruly student behavior. There are many strategies that can be implemented for this dilemma such as homogeneous groupings that insure these students are grouped in classrooms that don't include out of control students. This is my number one choice for resolving this dilemma. If you are a teacher who sees several groups of students a day, wouldn't it be simpler to see a group of disruptive students once a day instead of having them dispersed throughout every group you teach? It is simply unfair for respectful students to not be grouped together. If you are the parent of a respectful student, are you willing to do what it takes to insure your child is placed in a classroom with respectful students only? If you are the parent of a disrespectful student are you willing to admit that your child should not be allowed to prevent respectful students from learning and should be placed in a different classroom that's designed to provide the help your child needs? It is absolutely not fair for a teacher to have to figure out what to do with one disrespectful child at the expense of the rest of a group of students.

I will admit that a homogeneous group of disruptive students can be challenging. But, one factor that has worked in many cases is the fact that, in many schools where this has been implemented, affected students generally know they've been grouped this way and many will rise to the occasion and do what it takes without too much intervention to be able to return to a general population of good classrooms.

There are many strategies that can be implemented for homogeneous groups of unruly students. This is a situation where team teaching strategies could prove to be very effective, especially if these groups are placed on a block or self-contained schedule. A well structured program for how teachers and volunteers can work together to reduce a ratio of teacher to students, etc. could also prove to be effective as these students get the help that they need.

Regardless of what decisions are made, respectful students deserve the best we have to offer and they absolutely don't deserve to be in classrooms with out of control students. Adults in charge (parents, teachers, etc.) must be willing to become partners in implementing solutions for this dilemma. It's not fair to hear a respectful student make the following statement at the end of a school year.

"I got an A in Mrs. Wright's class but I didn't learn very much because there were too many kids who acted bad everyday in her room."

•Role 7: The Disrespectful Student •

Skit: "LET!"

Characters: Teacher / Mr. Forest Student / Chantelle

Setting

Mr. Forest enters the classroom from hall duty and closes the door as the tardy bell rings. Several students are out of their seats laughing and playing. Mr. Forest yells when he asks students to sit down. Fifteen minutes of instructional time is lost by the time students finally cease disruptive behavior. Mr. Forest is observably upset as he admonishes students for unruly behavior.

Scene

Mr. Forest
I don't understand why you come in here everyday with this nonsense! You waste at least fifteen minutes everyday and make it difficult for me to teach the lesson I planned to teach!

Chantelle
Mr. Forest we aren't learning anything in this classroom! All you do is yell and *LET* kids play the whole hour everyday!

Mr. Forest
LET?? LET kids play? I don't remember giving nobody in here permission to play! As for you Ms. Ring Leader Chantelle, if I *LET* myself write a referral on you and *LET* you walk out the room and carry this referral down to the principal's office, that will give me a chance to *LET* the rest of the class hear me when I teach the lesson!

Chantelle
Mr. Forest you can't talk about me like that!

Mr. Forest (*quickly quiet down*)
Okay! Then *LET* me quietly write this referral while I *LET* you prepare to leave the room. You're overdue…and I hope that in a day, or two, or three, or four, or five, or more, you will have resolved your behavior issues so I can…….***LET you back in this classroom!***

Sound familiar? I find it interesting that to this day, students will still repeat similar statements that place blame on a teacher as if the teacher gave students permission to misbehave. Unruly students are the real culprits in all of the mess. Personally speaking, I would have no reason to write this book if the behavior of these students cease to exist like dinosaurs.

The important question today is, can parents, teachers, administrators, etc. finally come to an agreement that in general, unruly students are consistent with their efforts to disrupt classrooms and play those of us who are in charge against each other if we do nothing to stop the behavior. Yes, if unruly behavior goes unchecked, these students become more and more creative with ways they misbehave. I will take it a step further by saying that they are like out of control actors who *perform* for an entire school year, refresh themselves while on summer vacation then come back and do the same thing all over again for another entire school year. Is it a wonder that so many students, including respectful students, fall behind year after year in accomplishing desired educational goals? Is it a wonder that so many respectful students get tired of being respectful when they are exposed to disrespectful students for long periods of time and finally give up by jumping on the *disrespectful student band wagon*? The following excerpt comes from my second classroom management book, When Kids Don't Listen. This is an exercise I did with eighth grade students when I taught school.

Excerpt

There's an exercise I did with my students to reiterate the magnitude of damage that results from long term inappropriate student behavior. In this exercise students were asked to discuss the importance of utilizing time effectively in a classroom. Students and I agreed that the average class period was approximately fifty minutes. We also decided that twenty days was the average number of days a month spent in school. I asked students to determine the amount of learning that might be accomplished in twenty days. The discussion was wonderful. They concluded that a great deal of learning could be accomplished in one month. They were then asked to determine the average length of time wasted in a classroom where unruly behavior is displayed daily. They had no difficulty responding to this request. On average most students said fifteen to fifty minutes was wasted as a result of unruly behavior. Then, I informed them we were going to take a look at how much time was lost in one school year if only ***five minutes*** *a class period was wasted due to poor behavior. They were asked to use pencil and paper to calculate results. This is what they were instructed to write.*

5 minutes ×5 days=25 minutes a week
25 minutes ×4 weeks=two 50 minute class periods a month
2 class periods ×10 months=20 class periods
Total: 4 weeks a school year wasted in a classroom due to poor behavior

When the exercise was completed, many students appear to be amazed at the fact that the final calculations for wasted class time were based on a mere five minutes per class session. Students were then given an opportunity to work in groups to calculate more realistic number for actual time wasted in classrooms. The results were astounding. Immediately following the exercise I saw an improvement in the behavior of some students that lasted the rest of the semester. Several students actually started admonishing unruly students to chill so they could learn. The exercise clearly demonstrated why some of the best students fall behind year after year. There are teachers who continue to utilize a sympathetic approach for instruction and therefore base instruction on overall student academic abilities for a group of students. This is a major problem in too many classrooms where students with high academic abilities are in the minority. In these classrooms instruction continues to be watered down to accommodate a majority of students who are usually behind in academic skills.

It's of utmost importance that teachers in this situation implement a classroom management strategy that will take care of this problem. A great majority of students who misbehave usually make the decision to do it prior to entering a classroom. Some children come to school behaviorally prepared to learn only to fall into poor behavior patterns as a result of peer pressure from students. If unchecked, poor behavior continues to escalate in classrooms throughout the nation as unruly students get better and more creative with ways they act out and disrupt classrooms. I included a sample list of unruly behaviors displayed in the second classroom management book I wrote and I'll repeat it here. Much of this behavior has been categorized by school administrators who are in charge of resolving student behavior issues as minor disruptive behavior. It's common knowledge that what some educators refer to as minor disruptive behavior constitute the majority of behavior problems occurring in classrooms. The list of problems is endless as disruptive students become more creative with what they can do to prevent teachers from teaching and students from learning. A sample list might look like this.

1. *excessive talking, chewing food items, chewing rubber bands or other objects*
2. *yelling out in class, using profanity, arguing with another student, jumping in front of students or jumping over student desks*
3. *reading or writing material or information that doesn't pertain to the class*
4. *telling a teacher to mind his/her own business when reprimanded for unruly behavior*
5. *sleeping and snoring in class*
6. *throwing supplies across the room to another student*
7. *throwing objects in the room*
8. *sliding objects across the floor to another student*
9. *entering without supplies but wearing headphones connected to a CD player*
10. *attempting to trip a student who has permission to walk to the pencil sharpener or other area of the classroom*
11. *displaying a poor attitude and refusing to answer a question asked by a teacher*
12. *telling a teacher that an administrator or parent won't do anything to correct a behavior problem*
13. *daring a teacher to give them failing grades*
14. *telling a teacher a failing grade won't prevent him/her (student) from being promoted*

The list is truly endless and much of the behavior goes unchecked as a result of minimizing the extent of disruptions to the learning process when the behavior occurs.

End of Excerpt

Let's take a good look at the overall situation with education in this country today. Some things really haven't changed. Money is still being spent to educate students. Parents still send children to school to receive an education. Teachers still attempt to teach students (and in many instances are quite successful so we won't forget that).

School administrators still require that school staff have regularly scheduled staff meetings to strategize on better ways to educate students. We also see an increasing trend towards implementation of longer school days and school years for students. All of these things are taking place in education as disruptive students who elect (yes elect) to misbehave continue to do everything they can think of to sabotage efforts to provide quality educational opportunities for students. The result is much of what we see in education today, too many uneducated or undereducated students that include respectful students who don't get the opportunity to receive a quality education in a timely manner.

I accept that my description of unruly student behavior is quite graphic but, so is the behavior. Those of us who are in charge are overdue to face reality and, if applicable, stop watering down the problem as if it's everyone's fault but the actual students who are causing disruptions. The bottom line is, we who care and who can make a difference are overdue to come together and form well structured partnerships that can address the problems. If applicable, it's time for those of us who haven't already done so to stop petty bickering over who is at fault for the problems and make informed decisions on how to work together. Otherwise unruly students will continue their quest knowing that a great majority of them will be socially promoted into the next grade level when a school year ends. It will be years later before many of them personally experience the effects of the damage their behavior has caused. Then, unfortunately many of them will become parents who will continue the cycle for the next generation of students. As a matter of fact, this has already happened for more than one generation of students. But, there is one thing that basically won't change for a majority of parents no matter what their behavioral background was in school. A majority of parents have the same expectations when they send their children to school which is:

"I send my child to school to learn. I expect the teacher to teach my child everything my child should know by the end of the school year!"

•Chapter 2 Summary•

It's time to do what it takes to resolve the discipline crisis that's running rampant in schools throughout the nation. It will take a team effort to resolve the crisis. Nothing less will do. Those of us who are in charge must increase our efforts to form partnerships that will allow us to work together in ways that make it clear to unruly students that we are in charge. Churches and other organizations must step up to the plate and be willing to consistently contribute to schools that are structurally sound and have organized plans on how to effectively utilize volunteers, monetary contributions, etc. If applicable, those of us who can make a difference must be willing to think and act past any walls, invisible or real, that confine our talents, contributions, etc. to one physical structure only such as, one church, one home, one school, one business, etc. Our efforts must also include strategies that will give students opportunities to become active participants in whatever is done to resolve the discipline crisis. Therefore, we must increase implementation of self-monitoring activities that allow students to monitor themselves in such a way that they take ownership of whether or not they violate rules established in classrooms, etc. Finally, we must develop a greater appreciation for the fact that a student's first classroom is in a student's home and behavioral strategies must be implemented that connect what happens in a student's home to what happens in schools. *'Don't Blame Me For The Mess'* must become an obsolete phrase for those of us who are willing to become members of that *one big team* that has a common goal of doing what it takes to improve educational opportunities for all students who are willing to respect educational environments.

•Suggested Follow Up Activities•

If you are a participant in a group of people who are reading this book, consider working with the group to plan workshops, group discussions, etc. that can be held in schools, churches or other locations for school staff only, parents only, school staff and parents, school staff, parents and volunteers, etc. Discuss information presented in this chapter and eventually, the entire book. Some suggested strategies are:

- Survey responses to question number one at the beginning of the chapter to determine who was selected as most responsible, second most responsible, etc. Discuss findings.

- Revisit the survey questions and your answers at the beginning of the chapter. Discuss whether or not your answers are the same after reading the chapter and why.

- Discuss your thoughts, opinions, conclusions, etc. about information presented in the chapter.

- Discuss how information presented in the chapter can be used to enhance the formation of teams and/or partnerships between people, institutions, etc.

- Discuss how information in this chapter can be used to improve existing student behavior strategies or develop new ones for use in schools and/or homes.

- Extend the discussion of different roles in this chapter by developing role playing activities that can be acted out by participants in a workshop, group discussion, etc. Demonstrators (performers) should really *get into character* for each role so that role playing reflects a pre and post mentality (negative and positive, etc.) for resolving the student behavior crisis. This can be very interesting and lots of fun.

If you are reading the book without participating in a workshop or interacting with other people, you have an opportunity to decide how to use the information presented in this book. There are several options that include, if applicable, using the information to improve a child or children's behavior in a home, presenting the book to a school, teachers, parent groups, churches, etc. It is my hope that I've written this book in such a way that options on how it can be used will be unlimited and will go way beyond strategies I've presented in the book.

"This is my prayer!"

Now it's your turn to write ideas, suggestions, conclusions, etc. Enjoy!

YOUR CONCLUSIONS, SUGGESTIONS, IDEAS, ETC.

3

Lights! Camera! Action!

In chapter two I discussed roles of different people, institutions, etc. that are involved or can become involved in making contributions to improve educational opportunities for students. However, there is one thing that hasn't changed very much over the years. The people who are generally on the front line when it comes to educating students in schools are classroom teachers. Therefore, helping individual teachers will continue to be a major topic when classroom management is discussed or written about.

When I hear or see the words *classroom management* I automatically think about teachers who do what it takes to be good role models for students in classrooms. However, I also think about parents who do what it takes to be good role models for children in homes. I then remind myself of what I consider to be similarities for both roles. For example, I've seen and experienced enough as a classroom teacher and educational consultant to know it's more effective and less stressful to talk in a calm manner than to yell when interacting with a group of students. I'm aware that there are many teachers who have developed a habit of talking loud or yelling in classrooms and therefore, many of these teachers do not agree with me. Some teachers explain the behavior by saying that there are too many students who don't pay attention to teachers who talk in a calm manner. In my work as a consultant there have been several occasions when I've suggested that individual teachers talk to a group of students the same way they would talk to a respectful child at home. I've been reminded by more than one teacher that there's a big difference between interacting with his/her child at home and interacting with groups of students in school. But, I've always said and will continue to say that a paradigm shift is in order and that the focus should be shifted from emphasizing differences to emphasizing similarities between the two roles. Because, if a teacher is also a parent who interacts with his/her child or children at home in a calm and respectful manner and it's working, the teacher should do likewise with groups of students in school and believe that the results can be the same for students.

There's a statement that I've repeated several times to teachers who talk extremely loud or yell in classrooms. I'm sure that I'll say it many more times before I cease working as a classroom management consultant. The statement: *"You are only one person. So no matter how loud you talk or yell, your students can talk louder and yell louder because there are more of them than you. So it's simply more practical to make them accountable for hearing you speak in a calm voice."* I believe this should be done by both teacher and parent to be good role models for students.

There are many wonderful examples that can be used to demonstrate similarities in the roles of teachers and other adults who are in charge of managing groups of people. For example, I can use the role of a play director to demonstrate similarities in the roles of a teacher and a play director.

<u>Showtime!</u>

<u>7:58a.m.</u>

It is two minutes to curtain time! Act I, Scene I is about to begin. The stage is a large classroom where all scenes will take place. The play is being looked at by a promoter (administrator) who will determine whether or not the play will have a long or short run. It's now one minute before the curtain opens! Is the stage (classroom) in order? Did the director (teacher) prepare an excellent script (classroom management plan) for the play's first scene? Is the director (teacher) ready to direct actors (students) when the curtain (door to classroom) opens? It's curtain time and the curtain slowly opens! Countdown....3....2....1!!! Lights!.....Camera!....Action!

<u>3:00p.m.</u>

The play has come to an end. Did actors (students) do a superb job following the script (classroom management plan) or, did they perform poorly? Was this an excellent play that the promoter (administrator) will support and tell others about or will the promoter (administrator) pull the plug (get another teacher)?

If you are a classroom teacher, which scenario represents your classroom? Is your classroom like a good play that school administrators are proud to invite visitors to see or, is it the dreaded classroom that they avoid at all costs when escorting visitors around the school? It is a question that only you can answer.

Yes you, the classroom teacher, have the power to decide what the answer will be!

This example clearly shows that the roles of a teacher and a play director are similar. For example, T.J. Hemphill (my brother) was the director and producer of his gospel hit play *Perilous Times* that was performed throughout the 1990's at The Music Hall Theatre in Detroit, Michigan. As one of the pianists for the play, I had many opportunities to observe him direct play rehearsals. Everyone involved in the play, actors, musicians, etc. understood what was expected of them. Actors knew their roles on and off stage and understood the consequences for not performing according to expectation. It was clear that the director was in charge and boundaries were established for everyone involved in the play. Actors were given some freedoms of expression but the limits of those freedoms were clearly defined.

When students enter a classroom they should be met by a teacher who is as prepared as an excellent play director. A teacher should be an excellent *director of scenes* that occur throughout a school year. The classroom is a *stage* where students will *perform*. It should be attractive with exciting bulletin boards that immediately capture students' attention. *Acts* and *scenes* that occur throughout the school year should have definitive beginnings and endings (clearly stated rules, responsibilities, expectations, etc.). Students should be aware at all times that they are interacting with a *no nonsense* teacher who is in charge of a well-structured educational environment. As a result, students will have opportunities to display their talents as they increase their knowledge.

A teacher who is behaviorally prepared to be a good role model for students will have the best opportunities to accomplish what needs to be done to effectively manage student behavior and educate students. There are two components that I believe it's crucial for a teacher to be aware of at all times. The components are a teacher's *demeanor* (in particular body language and facial expressions) and *vocal tone*. It's been proven that in general, students are very good at analyzing a teacher's demeanor at any given point in time and making a decision about whether or not they must *respectfully* follow a teacher's instructions. For example, students will study a teacher's *facial expressions* to determine what responses are appropriate for specific behaviors. When disruptive behavior occurs and a teacher reacts negatively by looking distraught and/or uncertain about how to handle a disruption, disruptive students will probably continue the disruption. If a teacher's reaction is positive and firm, students usually respond accordingly and cease disruptive behavior. A teacher who then follows up a disruptive occurrence by calmly but firmly discussing or implementing established consequences for applicable students can strengthen his/her position even more as being a good manager of student behavior.

A teacher's *vocal tone* is just as important as a teacher's physical demeanor. I cannot stress this enough. A teacher's speaking voice should sound calm and in control at all times. My motto was *"I would talk at all times as I wanted students to talk to me and each other."* I demonstrated an appropriate speaking level and informed students I'd rarely ever talk above that level. In my classroom it was always apparent when students were out of control because *I wasn't part of the problem*. I realize that today it has become more difficult to maintain control of one's temper when interacting with students who use profanity as if it's acceptable language. However, a teacher must remember that he/she should be a role model for students and therefore should commit to demonstrate by his/her actions how students should interact with the teacher and other people.

Therefore, there's a question that I believe is of utmost importance for teachers to being willing to answer. The question: *"Are you willing to see and hear yourself as students see and hear you?"* My work for the past eight years has taken me into many schools and classrooms. I've had the opportunity to see a multitude of teachers whose behavior was not conducive to educating students. I've heard several teachers yell at or argue with unruly students without regard for how respectful students or students in nearby classrooms were affected by the behavior. I actually give partial credit to several teachers for the title of this book because I've heard and continue to hear many teachers say, "*These Kids Have Changed!*" For some reason, these four words seem to provide a form of justification or summary statement for many teachers who simply accept the expression as a fact of life and settle into a routine of behavior that is unhealthy for teachers and students. Well, I will admit that many kids have changed and the changes have been negative. But there are still kids who make positive changes that make them better students and teachers need to focus more on the behavior of these students. The phrase, *These Kids Have Changed* doesn't have to imply negative change only.

There are many strategies that can be implemented by teachers who desire to become better role models for students. Although I've spent years in education, I also have years of experience as an entertainer. I've studied and performed as a vocalist and pianist. When I studied vocally one of my vocal exercises required that I look in a mirror and watch my body movements as I practiced assigned vocal exercises to insure certain things were or weren't happening physically. For example, my shoulders should not move up and down when I practiced breathing exercises. I also used a tape recorder so I could hear if the quality of my voice was improving over time as I continued to practice. One day, many years ago, I was practicing daily vocal exercises when I suddenly realized that these exercises could be applied to what a teacher needs to do to improve his/her overall demeanor and vocal tone. This resulted in me developing and recommending a strategy that I refer to as **mirror-tape exercises**. I developed the strategy and presented it to teachers I mentored by having each teacher do the following:

- Step 1: Write a list of negative statements that you (the teacher) use when interacting with disruptive students.

- Step 2: Write a list of positive statements that can be used to correct the negative statements.

Positive statements should emphasize student responsibility for correcting inappropriate behavior. For example, a statement commonly used by teachers who respond to students who are out of their seats without permission is; *"I told you to sit down."* A response I preferred to use was; *"I don't remember telling you to get out of your seat. You may be seated. Thank you."* My response reinforced the fact a student did not have permission to get out of his/her seat. I also spoke calmly but firmly and sat, stood or walked with good posture when I responded to unruly students. My students understood that I meant business and that I took issue with the fact that a rule was violated.

- Step 3: When you are ready to practice, position yourself in front of a mirror with a tape recorder nearby. Turn the tape recorder on and say one of the negative statements as you watch yourself in the mirror. Repeat the statement until it sounds like you do when you're in the classroom. Be honest with yourself and try to look and sound the way you do when you make the statement to students. When this has been accomplished, take a few minutes to think about the stress your body experiences when this behavior occurs in the classroom. Then, using the mirror and tape recorder again, practice the positive statement you selected to correct the negative response. Observe yourself in the mirror as you practice so you can see and hear how you want to look and sound the next time a disruption occurs and this response can be utilized. If necessary, correct your posture as you practice. Pay attention to whether or not you have a tendency to sit or stand in a non-authoritative or slumped position. After practice, play the tape back and analyze your practice. Make a commitment to write negative-positive statements as needed and practice regularly until you obtain your goal. In time you should develop the ability to spontaneously think of and utilize more appropriate responses when interacting with unruly students.

As I've stated before, the consultant work I do today started during the years I taught mathematics in middle school. During that time some of my co-workers utilized the mirror-tape exercises. I requested feedback from all teachers who used the exercises. I received verification from teachers who were willing to practice and evaluate themselves. It was these teachers who experienced the greatest success in their efforts to improve. They realized an effective teacher is one who's willing to acknowledge shortcomings. They accepted that they were not perfect, that they had a responsibility to behave better to affect positive changes in unruly student behavior and they went home and did their homework. In other words, they made the commitment to write statements as often as necessary and practice the mirror-tape exercises as needed to improve their skills to manage student behavior. There was also another factor that influenced the decision of these teachers to try this exercise. They accepted the fact that it was better they see and hear themselves and make needed corrections before being observed by an administrator who would see and hear them but, who may not be willing to give them the time needed to correct observed behavior.

If you are a teacher who needs work in this area, please take time now and list some of the negative statements you've made. Then list positive statements that you'd rather make to improve your ability to be a good classroom manager. (Reminder: Although this chapter focuses on a teacher's experience in a classroom, parents, etc. can also write statements as needed. Again, the teacher's experience is being used as an example for anyone who interacts with or instructs kids and who desires to develop, improve or reinforce skills to manage the behavior of kids in schools, homes, etc.)

Negative Statements	**Positive Statements**
Example: I told you to sit down!!	Correction: I don't remember telling you to get out of your seat!!
____________________	____________________
____________________	____________________
____________________	____________________
____________________	____________________
____________________	____________________
____________________	____________________
____________________	____________________
____________________	____________________

Now you have an opportunity to use your statements to practice the mirror-tape exercises. I encourage you to do this and to collaborate with others to strengthen your skills, evaluate your progress, etc.

In recent years I've also developed what I refer to as a **classroom management checklist**. I've used this checklist as a diagnostic and/or evaluative tool for school principals who've requested written information concerning my work with teachers. I developed the checklist to focus on three key areas. The areas are:

- classroom appearance
- implementation of a well-written discipline plan
- overall student behavior inside and outside a classroom

I've prepared two checklists that can be completed at this time, one for a teacher and the other for a parent. Again, parents and teachers are generally most directly responsible for educating students.

If you are a teacher please do a self-evaluation by completing the checklist on page 46.

If you are a parent please do a self-evaluation by completing the checklist on page 47. However, you should also review the teacher's checklist on page 46 because it will provide you with detailed information that's critical for teachers who desire to implement an effective classroom management plan. You can then decide how to use the information you obtain from both checklists. For example you may decide to discuss both checklists during a parent's group meeting. You may also decide to discuss the teacher's checklist with one or more teachers for the purpose of forming a partnership with teachers, etc.

Both checklists can be shared with many people. Therefore, blank checklist forms are located in the supplement (back of book).

CLASSROOM MANAGEMENT CHECKLIST (teacher)

Classroom Appearance	Excellent	Good	Need Improvement
teacher's desk			
bulletin boards			
student desks, tables, etc.			
bookcases, shelves, etc.			
Chalkboard			
Floor			
door			
windows & surrounding area			
other:			

Discipline Plan	Yes	No	Need Improvement
written discipline plan implemented in the classroom			
written discipline plan effective in classroom			
written discipline plan implemented in the hall area (hall duty, escorting students, etc.)			
written discipline plan effective in hall area			
teacher appears relaxed			
teacher's talking level is good			
teacher comments are effective when responding to inappropriate student behavior (non-repetitive, etc.)			
discipline plan includes opportunities for students to see their behavior patterns in writing			
administrator/s provided with written copy of discipline plan upon request			

Student Behavior	Excellent	Good	Need Improvement
movement in classroom is good			
all student movement in the classroom is monitored by the teacher			
movement outside of classroom is good			
student movement in the hall area is monitored by the teacher			
objects on student desks, tables, etc. are approved and appropriate for lesson/s			
students' talking level is good			
students talk by permission only			
students follow teacher instructions			
students are engaged in lesson/s			
learning centers implemented			
cooperative learning activities implemented			

COMMENTS

CHECKLIST FOR PARENT/S (home monitoring)

Discipline Plan	Yes	No	Need Improvement
you've explained rules that you expect your child/children to follow			
your child/children consistently follow rules you've established			
you've given instructions on how your child/children should complete assigned tasks in the home			
you've verified that your child/children understand how to complete assigned tasks in the home			
your child/children consistently complete assigned tasks in the home			
you are relaxed when interacting with your child/children who display disrespectful behavior			
your talking level is good when interacting with your child/children who display disrespectful behavior			
your comments are effective when responding to disrespectful behavior displayed by your child/children (non-repetitive)			
you are willing to work with your child's/children's teachers to implement and/or reinforce student behavioral expectations in school			

•Chapter 3 Summary•

If you are participating in a workshop session you may elect at this time to discuss information that's been recorded in this chapter with workshop participants.

If you are a teacher and you plan to practice the mirror-tape exercises, keep a log of your practice sessions, evaluate your sessions and adjust your practice sessions accordingly. Consider following up your practice sessions by selecting a co-worker who's willing to observe your interactions with students in the classroom and critique your efforts to improve. Observation by a co-worker can help you prepare for observation by an administrator. Remember, behaviors don't change overnight. Be persistent with your practice. Have patience and realize that your efforts for self-improvement may minimize the potential for having a stroke, heart attack, etc. Learn to accept what you can and can't do and don't dwell on people, issues, etc. you have no control over.

I accepted what I could and couldn't do years ago and developed my classroom management plan accordingly. I acknowledge that the phrase, *these kids have changed,* is generally not used by people to reflect positive change. But my response to this phrase is that it can reflect positive change but, if it doesn't, I'm saying, *where there's a will there's a way.* Therefore, if change is needed, I will continue to believe that those of us who are in charge have the power to do what needs to be done to affect positive change in student behavior.

The following *I Can Do* and *I Can't Do* list is being provided as a conclusion for chapter 3. Lines are provided for you (parent, teacher, etc.) to continue the list.

•I CAN DO and I CAN'T DO list•

This is a sample *I Can Do and I Can't Do* list. Continue the list by writing brief statements of student behavior related, incidents, situations, etc. that have caused you concern. Clarify what you can and can't do to resolve each incident. Keep in mind that it's wiser and more effective to utilize your energy for situations you can affect change upon. Wasting time blaming others for problems, etc. will divert your attention from implementing strategies that can accomplish the main goal of this book, to improve student behavior. Add statements to the list as needed to help you improve your ability to implement strategies for more effective management of a student's behavior in a home and /or a school.

SAMPLE LIST

I Can Do	I Can't Do
· control my behavior	· control the behavior of parents or administrators
· hold students accountable for following rules	· make parents hold their children accountable for following rules
· be calm, organized and consistent when documenting unruly student behavior	· make administrators suspend unruly students from school

---

I Can Do	I Can't Do

Reminder: Ola Hemphill's original classroom management plan is the basis for all revisions presented in this book. Therefore, chapter 4 should be read to insure a thorough understanding of the entire plan.

4

Is It The Army, Navy or Air Force?

(Preparing Monitoring Charts)

Several years ago one of my students made the following comment about the classroom management plan I implemented. She said, *"Ms. Hemphill, you act like we're in the army."* My *humorous* response to her was, *"That's right! All I need is a uniform and a pair of combat boots!"* My students, including the girl who made the comment, responded with laughter. I found myself doing likewise. This was not unusual because I enjoyed interacting with students and there were many times when laughter was followed by students paying better attention as I taught a lesson. As years passed, this kind of interaction with students enhanced my efforts to implement instruction by facilitating more and lecturing less.

To be or not to be a facilitator or lecturer! That is the question! It really is the question. Lecturing is a style of teaching that continues to be used by teachers who are more comfortable with this approach to educating students. Many teachers believe that lecturing is conducive to maintaining order in classrooms. They also use this approach when attempting to resolve student behavior problems. I think it's fair to say that in many situations, *the more unruly students are lectured to, the less they listen.* I believe there are parents, teachers, administrators, etc. who can support this statement. So again, it's time for *new ways to think about old strategies* when addressing poor student behavior. As the saying goes, if you continue doing the *same old things*, you can expect to get the *same old results* that include unruly students who have become more verbally aggressive towards parents, teachers, administrators, etc. who use lecturing to reprimand students. Many unruly students simply let what's said go in one ear and out the other because they know that lecturing is the only consequence they will incur for displaying *repetitive* unruly behavior. Lecturing is a verbal approach to solving student behavior problems that many times would be better solved by utilizing a non-verbal and/or written approach. However, the fact remains that lecturing is a strategy that will continue to be used by many teachers, administrators, parents, etc. who prefer or feel more comfortable using this approach to resolve behavior problems with children.

What affect can a facilitative approach have on resolving student behavior problems? Well, I believe a facilitative approach is much more effective over time and can give a facilitator multiple opportunities to insure students assume responsibility for displaying appropriate behavior. Therefore, a facilitative approach to managing student behavior that's implemented by using a well-written classroom management plan can minimize the need to verbally reprimand students who display unacceptable behavior. The classroom management plan that's presented in this book is based on using a facilitative approach for implementation. My plan, **The Classroom Monitoring System**, may initially require more written work than usual because it involves systematically documenting student behavior information. But, I believe it's worth it's weigh in gold. As far as I'm concerned, a good classroom management plan lays the foundation for a teacher to be able to utilize a facilitative approach to implement effective instruction for students. The more a teacher moves in the direction of becoming a facilitator the more opportunities a teacher will have to implement individualized and/or small group instruction.

Although I didn't use the word *facilitator* in 1984 when I developed the plan, I eventually realized that this was the approach I utilized to develop it. I used a blank grid to create a **master chart** for each class of students I taught. A master chart contained names of all students in a class and was duplicated to eliminate the need to continuously write student names on additional charts. Duplicated charts were used to prepare monitoring charts that included a **discipline chart**. A discipline chart laid the foundation for being able to implement the use of other charts. I also developed a set of **behavior codes** and used these codes to monitor students' behavior on a discipline chart. (A master chart, discipline chart and behavior codes will be discussed in detail in this chapter.) I was already familiar with using charts to track math skills for students in grades 5-8 when I taught in a math lab from 1976-1984. Therefore it was quite simple to apply the charting approach to managing student behavior when I started teaching large groups of 7th and 8th grade students (approximately 35 students per class). Once I implemented the discipline plan, I realized I could set up charts to manage other student activities such as individualized assignments for advanced students, math game activities for all students and random activities such as assigning books for home use, sending information home, etc. Using a set of charts to monitor several activities gave me wonderful opportunities to thoroughly discuss a student's behavioral and academic progress with parents who attended parent-teacher conferences, etc. A set of charts combined with a grade book and math log for each group of students actually minimized the amount of talking I had to do during a parent-conference. (A math log will be explained in chapter 8.)

The Classroom Monitoring System has proven effective for many teachers who've read and utilized my book/s. It has now been revised so that it can be used to accomplish goals of any reader who desires to contribute to improving educational opportunities for students. However, the original discipline plan I developed and implemented in 1984 will always be included in any book I write. In this chapter I will demonstrate the use of several charts. However, chart examples are not limited to examples presented in this chapter or the remainder of the book. It is hoped that this will be just the beginning for parents, teachers, administrators, etc. who desire to implement all or some components of the plan presented in this book. All charts in this chapter are located in the supplement (back of book) for duplication as desired. Additional charts are also included to allow more options for chart usage (Do not write on charts located in the supplement.) Now, let's take a look at some examples.

•Preparing A Master Chart for A Group of Students•

Step one for creating a **master chart** is to make copies of the 8½ in. x 11in. grid located in the supplement. The grid consists of approximately 15 rows, 1 wide column and 19 narrow columns. Next, use duplicated copies to set up a master chart for a group of students by following these steps.

1. For a group of students, use the number of duplicated copies necessary to alphabetically write student names in the wide column. Write a group or class heading in the space above the wide column (example: grade, section #, etc.) The heading should be written on every duplicated copy used to set up a *master chart* for a group of students. Therefore, if it's necessary to use two or more duplicated copies to write names for a group of students, complete a *master chart set* (two or more pages) by numbering pages. (example: pg.1 of____, pg.2 of______, etc.) Do not write anything else on master charts.

2. Duplicate a master chart or master chart set as needed. If a master chart set is duplicated I recommend that each duplicated set be stapled together. Duplicate master charts can then be used to set up several student activities that include discipline charts, etc.

3. Student names on master charts should be updated as needed prior to duplicating additional charts. Update charts by crossing out names of dropped students and adding names of new students. If necessary, write new master charts. I did not hesitate to redo master charts as needed to maintain student names as alphabetically as possible. When necessary I prepared new charts after student count day when classes were leveled off. (approximately one month after the beginning of a school year.)

All chart sets for a group of students can be kept in one folder. When I taught school I used long manila folders. Each folder contained a seating chart stapled to the front of the folder. Folders should be kept in a location that's inaccessible to students. This is crucial for a discipline chart because there will probably be students who will attempt to destroy this chart if they have access to it. I kept my charts in a location that could be locked daily. However, there were years when I took the charts home daily. I also prepared discipline charts for substitute teachers to use during my absence and transferred recorded information to my set of charts when I returned from an absence.

•Preparing A Discipline Chart For Use By Teachers•

I consider a **discipline chart** to be the most important chart in a set of charts that can be developed to monitor student activities. As I stated before, effective implementation of this chart lays the foundation for being able to use a set of charts to monitor several student activities. A discipline chart is created by duplicating a master chart or master chart set. (Refer to Example 4-1; pg.59 as needed throughout this discussion.) A discipline chart can hold approximately four weeks of student behavior information if each narrow column represents a different date. The title, *discipline chart* (or a similar title), should be written at the top of the chart in large letters. A narrow column should be dated from left to right whenever the chart is used to write student behavior codes. Then write the date above the same narrow column on every page of a chart set. A dated column will give the reader an opportunity to identify students who display inappropriate behavior on that date as well as students who display excellent behavior.

A set of **behavior codes** is used to write abbreviated information on a discipline chart. (Refer to Example 4-2; pg.60 as needed to see behavior codes.) This allows for quicker monitoring and documentation of inappropriate student behavior as incidents occur. The result is that behavior information can be quickly documented for several students in a short period of time without writing lengthy statements. Additional codes should be added to a set of behavior codes as needed. For example, I added the **'SO'** code (sliding object on floor) to my list several years ago when a student slid a pencil across the floor to another student. **'WT'** (wasting time) was added when I realized that several parents were concerned about students who had fairly good attendance and didn't display disruptive behavior such as blurting out, etc., but, their math grades were not good. It became important to accurately display a *pattern of behavior* that clearly showed these students wasted an excessive amount of time in class.

After years of conducting classroom management workshops and mentoring several teachers, before going any further, I'd like to respond to a major concern several teachers have expressed. *It's not necessary to write down every single incident that occurs with every student who displays inappropriate behavior.* The purpose of a discipline chart is to document and establish a student's behavior pattern over a period of several days or weeks. Discipline charts for a group of students can contain several weeks of information, especially when two or three sets of charts have been filled in that contain nine or ten weeks of information. Therefore, if a student talks excessively, it's important to show several dates that this behavior has occurred even if the behavior was not documented every single time the student talked. A student's pattern of behavior will carry more weight than any single incident. Documented student behavior patterns insure that it's easy to identify students who have poor behavior patterns and also identify students who have good behavior patterns. When I implemented the plan most students were very concerned about what was documented on a discipline chart. Today I continue to get feedback from teachers who say likewise.

Students who display the most disruptive behavior in classrooms are usually part of a minority of students that many teachers identify as *ring leaders* for the majority of behavior problems that occur in classrooms. This was an important fact in the development of my plan because I believed that the plan would settle the behavior of a majority of students in a group so it would be easier to identify and document behavior of the most disruptive students. The most disruptive students in classes I taught settled down when students who didn't want to be documented avoided interacting with them. The plan was definitely effective and consistent implementation of it combined with my efforts to *maintain good behavior on my part* decreased the need to verbally interact with students to correct behavior problems. Students knew what *the look* meant (a certain look I displayed when a behavior problem occurred) and they knew what *heading towards or picking up the chart* meant. The fact that a student's behavior pattern could immediately be documented and compared to other students was a win-win for a majority of students who were responsive to the plan and it gave me opportunities I needed to document and address the behavior of the most disruptive students.

Another concern that has been expressed by teachers in recent years is that during a parent-teacher conference, etc. names of all students on a discipline chart are exposed to whoever is reading the chart. To resolve this concern I suggested that the narrow column to the left and to the right of students' names be used to number each student. During a conference a chart can then be folded to expose numbers to the right only as a teacher is aware at all times which student is being discussed. The peer pressure factor will still exist as a student's behavior pattern can be compared to behavior patterns of other students on the chart even when names are not exposed. The discipline chart example in this book is not numbered as such because it represents the original chart that I used and I didn't feel the need to hide student names during the years I taught school.

Now, let's take a look at example 4-1; pg.59 to get a better understanding of the benefits of being able to compare student behavior patterns. Select the two students who appear to have the worst behavior patterns then return to this page to continue reading. If you choose the students chosen by most people your choices are, number one worst student is Brenda Jones and number two is Yolanda Lewis. Now go back to example 4-1 and choose the best two students then return back to this page to continue reading. If you choose the students chosen by most people your choices are, number one best is Sheila Jones and number two is Todd Abrams. It's extremely important that you use the behavior of respectful students to get everybody on track. Therefore, respectful students should never be ignored. But it's also important that you don't necessary name these students in a classroom unless you determine their safety is not jeopardized by unruly students who may attempt to harm them due to jealousy, etc. There are many comments that can be utilized to describe the behavior of respectful students such as, *"There's at least eight students who have no behavior codes next to their names. I'm so proud of these students."* Believe me when I say, the majority of students in a group know who these students are although no names have been mentioned. That statement can immediately be followed up with one such as, *"If you are not one of these students, you certainly have an opportunity to show on this chart that your behavior has improved. The less I write in your student boxes on the discipline chart, the more empty boxes you will have to verify that your behavior has improved."*

A discipline chart is easy to use. When a behavior problem occurs, date the first available narrow column to the right of students' names. If more than one page is stapled to create a chart set, date the same column on all pages. Do not date the chart on days when there are no behavior problems. Locate a student's box in a dated column and write behavior codes that correspond to behavior displayed. (**T** for talking, **AO** for accepting an object, **DN** for disruptive noise, etc.) Example 4-1 shows it's possible to write four or five behavior codes in one box. Several of my former co-workers wrote small enough to write more than five. Example 4-1 shows how several students in section 8-4 were documented for rule violations. See the column dated 9/27. (September 27th) Student Yolanda Lewis was documented for displaying poor behavior. See the column dated 10/28 for student Brenda Jones who also displayed poor behavior. Two columns were used to document Brenda's behavior. Also notice the word **"over"** is written in Brenda's box. Brenda's behavior resulted in a written referral to an administrator. Information is documented on back of the chart. This is important when it's necessary to recall details (see Example 4-1; back of chart for 10/28).

When a student is referred to an administrator a circled ® representing referral should be written in the student's box. Write a brief description of the information on back of the chart. Remember to write the word **"over"** to show information is written on back of the chart. I used a red pen to write the word **"over"** and ®. Over the years I've encountered teachers who utilized space more efficiently by using symbols such as check marks, etc. to represent the word **"over"**, etc. Keep a copy of a referral that's sent to an administrator. (Today I still recommend use of carbon paper when necessary to avoid sending a referral that has not been duplicated to an administrator.) When you receive a disposition from an administrator attach it to your copy of the referral. If no disposition is received, write information on the copy you kept for future reference.

The effort should be made to minimize referral writing. I rarely wrote more than five to ten a semester. I was consistent about documenting poor behavior on a discipline chart. Students were amazed at my ability to consistently document poor behavior even under the worst circumstances. They quieted down when they realized I was serious about establishing poor student behavior patterns in writing. If you are a new teacher in a school a discipline chart will probably be used more during your initial interactions with students. If you remain in a school for a substantial period of time students who also attend the school for a substantial period of time will become aware of your ability to manage or not manage student behavior. If you are a good manager of student behavior, your job will be made easier as students spread the news throughout the school about your ability to manage student behavior. It doesn't matter if students are happy about what you're doing or not. They will spread the news and it's up to you what it will be.

Consistency is the word for today, tomorrow and forever! Do not give students an opportunity to believe you are not maintaining a discipline chart. They *will* observe you for consistency. I recommend starting a new discipline chart each card marking period to give students an opportunity to start with a clean slate. It may be necessary to use more than one duplicated chart set a card marking period to continue documenting behavior information for a group of students due to the length of a marking period. Do not throw old charts away. Inform students that when it's necessary to write a referral you will transfer information from discipline charts to referrals. At strategic times discuss information contained on a discipline chart with individual students, particularly when there's an improvement in behavior. Always make sure each student is aware of how he/she ranks behaviorally in a class. It doesn't hurt from time to time to also comment on overall improvement in student behavior for an entire group of students.

Another strategy that's proven effective over the years is being used by several elementary teachers I've encountered. They post wall charts that are identical to a discipline chart except wall charts are larger and each column represents one week instead of one day. On a weekly basis they place symbols, colors, stars, etc. in student boxes to represent how well each student behaves for a week. The information written on discipline charts determines which symbols will be used. The more visual the information, the more students tend to be concerned about what's written, displayed, etc.

A **Letter/Codes Sheet** is used to prepare a summarized student behavior report for information contained on a discipline chart. (Refer to Example 4-2; pg.60 as needed throughout discussion of letter/codes sheet.) This sheet contains the set of behavior codes that are used to monitor student behavior in a classroom. The sheet also includes codes that represent a school's dress code (**D** codes) and codes that represented carrying food, beverages, etc. into classrooms, etc. (**C** codes). There are also additional lines provided on the sheet to add behavior codes.

Summarized student behavior reports can be prepared by duplicating the letter/codes sheet located in the supplement. (Reminder: Do not write on the original located in the supplement.) The following instructions describe steps for preparing letter/codes sheets for a group of students.

1. For each group of students duplicate one copy of the letter/codes sheet located in the supplement.

2. Complete the following information at the top of a duplicate copy: date, teacher, subject/hour, writing assignment number/s, due date, number of times. Then make duplicates of the partially completed sheet for students who need a behavior report mailed home. (one sheet per student)

3. Complete a student's letter/codes sheet by writing the student's name and transferring the student's behavior codes from a discipline chart onto the student's letter/codes sheet. (See example 4-2 for a sheet that was completed on Yolanda Lewis.)

4. After completing individual sheets make a duplicate set of all sheets. I suggest mailing one copy home for each student and keeping the other copy in a file.

During my teaching years I reserved the last two columns of a discipline chart to log information pertaining to mailing letter/codes sheets to parents. I mailed this information home once every card marking period. Therefore, there were card marking periods when I used two sets of discipline charts per group of students. When this occurred I wrote letter/codes sheet information in the last two columns on the second set of charts. (Review example 4-1 on pg.59. Example 4-1 has been abbreviated to include an example of logging letter/codes sheet information in the last two columns.) In the column prior to the last column I wrote the abbreviated heading **LM** for *letter mailed home* with a mailing date. I dated the column to show when I placed letters in a school pickup for mailing. I wrote an **X** in student boxes for all students whose parents would receive a letter. If a student's mailing date differed from the date at the top of the column, I wrote the mailing date in the student's box. I also prepared academic progress reports to be mailed home to parents. If a student needed both reports mailed home, they were placed in one envelope for mailing. This emphasized the fact that the reports were separate but equally important.

The information for mailing letter/codes sheets to parents was completed by writing the abbreviated heading **L/W ret.** in the last column of a discipline chart. The abbreviation means *letter and/or writing assignment returned.* A student's box was dated when he/she returned the writing assignment that was included on the letter/codes sheet. When a student returned a writing assignment and letter/codes sheet with parental signature, the writing assignment was disposed of. The letter/codes sheet was attached to the discipline chart or placed in an envelope or folder reserved for returned writing assignments and letter/codes sheets. If a parental signature was written on the writing assignment, the page containing the signature was attached to the duplicate copy of the letter/codes sheet and discipline chart or placed in a reserved envelope or folder. Students were informed that failure to turn in a writing assignment could result in the lowest citizenship mark possible. Review example 4-1 for Brenda Jones who did not return a writing assignment. Her student box is empty. Student Dan Farley returned his writing assignment on 11/25.

The writing assignment included on a letter/codes sheet was short but important. Example 4-2; pg.60 shows that I assigned numbers 1 and 2 to be completed and turned in. Students were required to write each numbered statement three times. Although I wanted students to read statements that reiterated their responsibility for displaying appropriate behavior, I wanted to eliminate a student complaining about too much to write. The writing assignment also minimized excessive paper work for me. How many times have you read through 10 pages of a writing assignment such as *'I will not chew gum'* to make sure the handwriting was that of the student assigned to write it? You probably had to go a step further and check to insure carbon paper wasn't used. An assignment of this type teaches very little. I believe it's important for teachers to minimize paper work that doesn't pertain directly to teaching.

When used together a discipline chart and letter/codes sheet are wonderful tools for monitoring and modifying poor student behavior. A short writing assignment is advantageous for parents who will not be required to read an excessive amount of information or possibly listen to a lengthy explanation if a teacher contacts the parent by telephone. Most parents are aware of their child's behavior pattern before a teacher encounters the child. By the time a child enters 1st grade the child's behavior pattern is generally *old news* for a parent. I chose not to waste time being repetitive. Therefore, I did not call parents. I focused directly on students by informing them at the beginning of a semester that I expected them to control their behavior. I made it clear that I would teach in an environment conducive to learning. If they disrupted that environment consequences would definitely include mailing a detailed student behavior report to a parent. Once reports were mailed home students were required to return writing assignments in a timely manner and show measurable improvement in their behavior before they could received an improved citizenship grade for an upcoming card marking period. Simply put, students were given this opportunity to wipe the slate clean for the next card marking period. When a student returned a signed letter/codes sheet, I destroyed the unsigned file copy and filed the signed copy.

The letter/codes sheet I developed became very popular during my teaching years and resulted in a second letter/codes sheet that did not contain student behavior codes. This sheet resulted from teachers requesting a copy of the sheet without student behavior codes. It gave a teacher the opportunity to create a set of behavior codes that was more relevant to behavior that occur in the teacher's classroom.

Co-workers who used my plan benefited greatly and made every effort to follow whatever I recommended to the letter. My instructions included reminding them to keep a discipline chart and one or two copies of a letter/codes sheet together in a folder for each group of students. It was important that a teacher have access to these items at all times for quick and effective monitoring of student behavior.

EXAMPLE 4-1 (front)

DISCIPLINE CHART

Section 8-4 Page 1 of 3	9/27	9/28	10/19	10/28	cont.	10/29		LM:11/17	L/W ret.
Abrams, Todd		O						—	—
Farley, Dan			T			PO DB OVER		X	11/25
Jones, Brenda		TH DN	DT	T W C TH	DT ® OVER			X	
Lewis, Yolanda	PO DN T	DT W O	DB OVER					X	11/24
Stewart, Janet						AO DB OVER		X	11/26
Washington, Brian	T C		T					—	—
Young, Sheila								—	—

CODE REMINDER: On 9/27 Yolanda Lewis was marked for:
PO-passing an object without permission
DN-disruptive noise
T-talking

WRITING ASSIGNMENT CODE:
LM-letter mailed
L/W ret.-Letter/Code Sheet and/or writing assignment returned with parental signature

---

EXAMPLE 4-1 (back)

(Discipline Chart:other side)

10/19 Yolanda: took paper from Brian without permission /parent-teacher-student conference scheduled for 10/23 (excessive violations)
10/28 Brenda: sent to Mr. Hamilton (administrator) for excessive violations
10/29 Dan and Janet: Dan passed pornographic drawing of male and female sex organs to Janet /log info on both Documentation Sheets

EXAMPLE 4-2

LETTER / CODES SHEET

Date: 11/17
Teacher: Mr. Jackson
Subject / Hour: Math / 4th

Student, Yolanda Lewis, must complete writing assignment number/s 1 and 2 as a result of inappropriate behavior. (see below)

Due Date: 11/30
Number of times: 3 each
Parental signature: ______

Writing Assignment

1. **Respect for staff persons**: Students must respect administrators, teachers and all staff persons. (custodians, lunchroom workers, etc.) Students must answer questions asked by a staff person.
2. **Respect for other students**: Students are responsible for avoiding behavior that is detrimental to the achievement of educational goals for all students. Students must refrain from destroying the property of others, name calling, verbal or physical threats, etc.

Behavior Codes

B-behavior
Bl-blatant
C-chewing
D-disruptive
Di-distracting
E-entrance
Ex-exit
F-fighting
H-hitting
I-insubordination
L-laughing
N-noise
O-out of seat
P-playing
R-running

S-standing
Sh-shoving
Sl-sleeping
T-talking
W-walking
AO-accepting an object
PO-passing an object
AS-attempting to sleep
FD-foot on back of desk
OF-objects on floor
NA-not paying attention
SO-sliding object on floor
TH-throwing an object
UI-unprepared for instruction
WT-wasting time

M1-missing pen or pencil
M2-missing paper
M3-missing textbook
D1-wearing a coat
D2-wearing a jacket
D3-wearing a hat
C1-carrying food
C2-carrying a beverage

Student's behavior pattern (transferred from Discipline Chart): **T** (*several times*), **DT, PO, DB, O, W, DN**

Other Comments: *parent-teacher-student conference scheduled for 10/23 (for excessive violations) / conference completed on 10/23*

•Preparing Monitoring Charts For Use By Parents•

The need to bridge the gap between strategies that are used to manage the behavior of students in homes and in schools is tremendous. There is a great deal of talk and many articles written about how important parental involvement is to effectively educate students. The need to find *new ways to think about old strategies* has resulted in me developing monitoring charts that parents can use in homes. I give credit to many teachers who've given me feedback that they or some of their co-workers have used my classroom management plan and reinforced its use by sending the letter/codes sheet I developed home so parents could familiarize themselves with the behavior codes. I've been informed that parents have been very appreciative of this information that has resulted in more productive parent-teacher conferences and improved behavior on the part of applicable students. Therefore, once I took time to re-evaluate my experiences as a teacher and a consultant for the past eight years, it wasn't difficult to modify my plan by developing charts for parents to use at home. It became clearer to me that we can't just talk about how important parental involvement is without recommending strategies that give parents opportunities to become more involved. I also believed it was important that recommended strategies emphasize bridging the gap between how parents manage student behavior, tasks, etc. in homes and teachers, administrators, etc. manage student behavior in schools.

A parent who reads this book and implements the plan in a home may reap the benefit of seeing a child's behavior improve at home and in school, especially if a parent forms a partnership with a teacher to enhance implementation of the plan. (Partnerships are discussed in chapter 5.) Understanding the plan presented in this book also gives a parent options that include being able to present it to schools, parent groups, etc. Classroom management plans for the most part are developed for and presented to educators. It's time to change this so parents are empowered to be able to present classroom management plans to schools for consideration of implementation. Therefore, for purposes of this book, parents should definitely understand the original classroom management plan I developed for teachers. This can be accomplished by reading the entire book or, at the least, by reading pages 50-60.

The first example for preparing a chart for parental use in a home is the same as preparing a discipline chart for use by teachers. Therefore, a parent can make duplicates of the 8½ in. x 11in. grid located in the supplement (back of book). A duplicate chart can then be used to prepare a chart to monitor the behavior of more than one child, monitor assigned tasks for more than one child, etc. (Continue to review pgs.50-60 as needed.) The duplicate chart should have a heading for the activity or activities that will be monitored. Date columns daily or as needed. Behavior codes or codes should be created as needed. For example, a set of codes can be created for cleaning a bedroom by using the letter **B** for bedroom and adding a number to the letter **B** that represents a certain task that need to be completed. (I thank two of my grandchildren for contributing to the development of codes for bedroom tasks located on page 62.) The same can be done for kitchen tasks by using the letter **K** with assigned numbers. The letters **Be** can be used with assigned numbers for personal behavior issues such as arguing with a parent, arguing with a sibling, responding disrespectfully to a parent, etc. It may even be simpler in some cases to assign numbers only for a chart specifically set up to clean one room only. (Example-a bedroom: **1**-make bed **2**-clean dresser **3**-vacuum floor) Again, the 8½ in. x 11in. grid located in the supplement can be used as desired and is excellent for monitoring the activities of several children, etc.

Bedroom Codes	**Kitchen**	**Behavior Codes**
B1 (make bed)	K1 (wash dishes)	Be1 (not following orders)
B2 (clean dresser)	K2 (dry dishes)	Be2 (arguing with parent)
B3 (vacuum floor)	K3 (put dishes away)	Be3 (arguing with sibling)
B4 (clean mirror)	K4 (clean stove)	B4 (disrespectfully talking back)
B5 (hang up clothes)	K5 (sweep floor)	
B6 (fold and put clean clothes in dresser		
B7 (put toys away)		
B8 (take dirty dishes out)		
B9 (clean door)		
B10 (wipe walls)		

•Preparing A Self-Monitoring Tasks Chart For One Child•

A self-monitoring chart is a multipurpose chart that can be prepared by a parent, teacher, administrator, etc. to monitor one or more activities for one or more children/students. Example 4-3 below shows that a parent has prepared the chart for one child who is assigned tasks to clean a bedroom. Codes for tasks to be completed are listed in the wide left column. The chart covers a two week period and includes the following five days for each week; Mon., Tues., Thur., Fri. & Sat. Tasks to be completed are coded and listed under dates in columns. (This is an abbreviated chart. The chart in the supplement covers a two week period and has columns for seven days each week.)

EXAMPLE 4-3

Self-Monitoring Chart: Child's Name ____________________________
Assignment: Clean Bedroom ____________________________
Assigned By: Parent's Name ____________________________

Progress Codes: **E**-Excellent **G**-Good **I**-Improved **P**-Poor

Bedroom Tasks	**Weekly Progress Code =**					**Weekly Progress Code =**				
	Mon. 9/9	Tues. 9/10	Thur. 9/12	Fri. 9/13	Sat. 9/14	Mon. 9/16	Tues. 9/17	Thur. 9/19	Fri. 9/20	Sat. 9/21
B1-make up bed B2-clean dresser B3-vacuum floor B4-clean mirror/s B5-hang up clothes B6-fold and put clean clothes in dresser B7-put toys away B8-take dirty dishes out B9-clean door B10-wipe walls	B1 B5 B8	B1 B3 B5 B8	B1 B2 B5 B7	B1 B5 B8	B1 B3 B6	B1 B5 B8	B1 B3 B5 B8	B1 B5 B7	B1 B5 B8	B1 B3 B4 B6 B9 B10

Example 4-3 shows several assigned tasks. A bed must be made up daily. Although Wednesdays and Sundays are not included on the chart, a parent, etc. can simply say that it's an expectation that these days are included for making up a bed. The chart shows that the child has been assigned to clean a dresser on Thursday of one week but not the other. The child has also been assigned to vacuum the floor on Tuesday and Saturday of both weeks.

There are many options for preparing and monitoring tasks. For example, a child can be given the opportunity to contribute to preparing the chart by using line or unlined paper to write tasks that need to be done to clean his/her bedroom. Whenever possible, I believe children should be allowed to participate in the planning stage/s of any behavioral strategies that will be implemented for the purpose of improving their behavior, improving their ability to complete tasks, etc. My grandchildren who made a contribution to preparing the bedroom tasks included on page 62 actually enjoyed the activity. After a child writes a list of tasks a parent can check the list and revise it as needed before tasks are written on a self-monitoring chart. Chart preparation can then be completed by listing codes/tasks in the wide left column of the chart, writing tasks to be completed in dated columns then duplicating the chart to provide one copy for a parent and the other for a child. A parent may elect to have a child select and write tasks in dated columns prior to duplicating charts. A parent can then request that a child circle tasks on his/her chart as they are completed. A parent can follow up by looking at the child's chart daily or weekly, comparing what's written on the child's chart to what's written on the parent's copy of the chart, etc. A parent may also write comments below or on back of the child's chart that explain or clarify the weekly code that the parent selects to show how well the child completes tasks.

Again, there are multiple options for how a self-monitoring chart can be prepared and used that include using erasable boards, markers, etc. instead of pen and paper, etc. Also, as I stated on page 62, it may be simpler to use numbers only to identify various tasks. If it is determined that a child will be assigned the same tasks weekly, a chart can be set up with assigned codes/tasks and duplicated to cover several weeks before writing on charts. Assigned tasks can then be added or deleted for upcoming weeks.

In the next example you will see how the same chart can be used by a teacher to implement a self-monitoring behavior chart for individual students.

•Preparing A Self-Monitoring Behavior Chart For Use By All Students In A Group•

This chart can be used by teachers to give students an opportunity to participate daily in a self-monitoring procedure. If applicable, it's time for students to tap into their inner selves and assume greater responsibility for paying attention to how they behave at any given point in time. Therefore, each student should have an immediate consequence for displaying unruly behavior. A self-monitoring behavior chart can serve the purpose of holding a student accountable for recording his/her unruly behavior immediately after it occurs. The ultimate goal is for a student to think before acting to avoid behavior violations that require a student document his/her own behavior. This chart does not replace a discipline chart that a teacher is using to monitor a group of students.

A teacher can prepare a self-monitoring behavior chart by making one duplicate copy of the blank self-monitoring chart provided in the supplement. (Refer to Example 4-4 on pg. 66 as needed.) Then write or type behavior codes & behaviors in the left wide column on the duplicate copy. After writing or typing behavior codes duplicate as many copies as needed (one copy per student). (Option: A sheet containing a set of behavior codes can be attached to each student's self-monitoring chart in lieu of writing or typing behavior codes on a self-monitoring chart.)

Example 4-4; pg.66 displays a self-monitoring chart that a student has been required to log behavior information on daily. If a teacher uses a discipline chart to monitor student behavior (this should be the case), students should understand that information written on self-monitoring charts should reflect what's written on a discipline chart. In other words, as previously stated, the goal is for a student to think before acting so that he/she can avoid any action that requires writing on a self-monitoring chart and being documented on a discipline chart. Students should also be informed that, if their behavior has been good or excellent for an entire class period, they can write something on their charts that represent good behavior such as: *My behavior was excellent today.* If nothing is written on a student's self-monitoring chart for a scheduled class period, it reflects good behavior. If a student displays unruly behavior and refuses to write information on a self-monitoring chart this should be documented as insubordinate behavior on a discipline chart. The back of a discipline chart should be dated followed by the student's name and a brief explanation of the problem. (In chapter 7 I will discuss implementation of an individualized documentation sheet for a student who displays extremely poor behavior.)

Implementation of a self-monitoring behavior chart has the potential to lighten a teacher's burden to monitor student behavior as students assume more responsibility for monitoring themselves throughout a class period. A teacher should reinforce the activity by giving students examples such as the following: *If a student displays inappropriate behavior, violates a rule, etc., ask the student if he/she wrote a behavior code on a self-monitoring chart.* Students should be reminded that information they write should coincide with what's written on a discipline chart being maintained by a teacher. This can be very important when meeting with an administrator and/or parent to discuss a student's behavior, what classroom management strategies are being implemented, etc.

Self-monitoring charts should be passed out at the beginning of each class period and collected prior to the end of the same period. If a student fails to turn in a self-monitoring behavior chart this should be documented on a discipline chart accompanied by a brief explanation written on back of a discipline chart. It's important that an administrator, parent, etc. is made aware that a student has the opportunity to self-monitor his/her behavior but refuses to do so. This behavior will probably be characteristic of a student who has chosen to display unruly behavior and has no intentions of *self-correcting* the behavior. I believe it's important that as we *find new ways to think about old strategies*, we can show that we are giving students opportunities to participate in what needs to be done to resolve student behavior problems. The result is that we clarify without a doubt whether or not a student has the right intentions when it pertains to displaying respectful behavior in classrooms, etc. There are multiple options for how this chart can be used daily that include passing out charts at the beginning of a class period to select students based on student behavior. If necessary, these charts should be passed out and collected by a teacher.

EXAMPLE 4-4 (front)

Self-Monitoring Chart: Robert Jones
Assignment: Monitor Behavior
Assigned By: Teacher's Name /Class

Progress Codes: **E**-Excellent **G**-Good **I**-Improved **P**-Poor

Behavior Codes	**Week 1: Progress Code= I**					**Week 2: Progress Code=**				
	Mon 9/9	Tues 9/10	Wed 9/11	Thur 9/12	Fri 9/13	Mon 9/16	Tues 9/17	Wed 9/18	Thur 9/19	Fri 9/20
(ex)-excessive **t**-talking **o**-out of seat **wt**-wasting time **na**-not paying attention **po**-passing an object **ao**-accepting an object	t (ex) o (ex) wt(ex) na	t wt (ex) na (ex)	wt (ex)	my behavior was excellent today	wt					

EXAMPLE 4-4 (back)

A student should write dates and statement as needed. This is an example for formatting information.

9/9: I apologize for my behavior and I promise to act better. I will do all my work and stop wasting time in class. I do not want to have to write on my chart everyday.

Example 4-4 (front) shows that student Robert Jones wrote four behavior codes in the column dated September 9th. On the back Robert wrote a commitment to do better. Robert's behavior improved by September 11th and on September 12th he wrote that he displayed excellent behavior.

There are many strategies, options, etc. on how a teacher can implement this chart that can include the following suggestions.

- Set up a chart for each student in a class (write student's name on chart). Pass charts out when students enter the classroom daily. Instruct students to write behavior codes on their charts as necessary to show when code violations occur. Inform students that behavior codes they write on their charts should reflect what you would write on a discipline chart for the class. They should also be instructed to write short statements on back of their charts if they display any behavior that requires additional information. Collect charts at the end of each class period or as needed from individual students. Clarify follow up procedures, consequences, etc. Also clarify that the purpose for using a self-monitoring behavior chart in class is so students will think before acting so they can avoid having to document behavior that violates rules, etc.

- Set up a chart for each student in a class. Require that only select students use the chart as necessary based on behavioral needs.

- Instruct students to review previously recorded information and strive to improve behavior as needed.

- Decide if you or a student will record a weekly progress code on a student's chart. For example, you may instruct students to record weekly codes on their charts. This will be followed up by you recording what the codes should actually be on a wall chart that's posted to show weekly progress for the entire group. Each column on the wall chart can be set up to show the codes written by you and a student. For example, a diagonal can be used to separate the code you wrote from the code a student wrote. <u>Example</u>: **E/G** where **<u>E</u>** represents the code you wrote and **<u>G</u>** represents the code a student wrote. Remind students that the goal is for the two codes to match, therefore reflecting that students are doing an excellent job of recording accurate behavior codes on self-monitoring charts.

Again, options for how a self-monitoring chart can be used are unlimited. It's of utmost importance that those of us who are in charge take the time that's needed to implement strategies that will give kids opportunities to assume more responsibility for *thinking before they act*.

•Monitoring Homework•

There are two more chart examples I've included in this chapter that address a major concern for parents, teachers, administrators, etc. The concern is, students completing homework assignments. I was always amazed that the majority of parents I encountered didn't ask what the daily class assignments were. They asked if a child had homework.
A common complaint many administrators encounter from parents is that certain teachers don't give enough homework. So I decided to create a homework chart and describe two examples for how the chart can be used. A homework chart can be implemented by a parent, a teacher, an administrator for an entire school, etc. to raise student accountability for completing homework assignments. Again, the more charts are used to verify completion of tasks, homework assignments, etc., the less parents, teachers, administrators, etc. will have to talk to verify completion of assigned homework, tasks, etc. Example 4-5 below shows how a student can log homework assignments. Example 4-6 on page 70 shows how a teacher can log assignments for a group of students. This chart can also be used by a parent to log homework assignments for two or more children, etc.

EXAMPLE 4-5

Homework Chart: __________________________________
(name)

Subject/s	Oct. 8	Oct. 9	Oct. 10	Oct. 11	Oct. 12	Homework Completion Codes						Homework Completion Codes					
Reading	X	X		X	X	E											
Language Arts		X		/		F											
Math	X		/		X	G											
Science		/		/	/	N											

Codes for Homework Chart Example 4-5

Assigned homework: one diagonal in a box

Completed homework: an X in a box

Homework Completion Codes: ·**E**-Excellent ·**G**-Good ·**F**-Fair ·**N**-Need Improvement

Example 4-5 shows dates that a student was assigned homework. It also shows dates homework was completed and/or turned in. There are multiple options for how this chart can be used by a teacher, parent, etc.

- A parent may decide to set up a chart per child and record information daily by asking a child if homework is assigned then verifying completion of the homework. At the end of a week a parent selects the homework completion code/s to use to finalize a child's progress for each subject listed on a homework chart.

- A parent may decide to set up two charts per child and require that a child record homework information as homework is assigned and completed. A parent then has the option to transfer information recorded by a child onto a parent's copy of the same chart.

Example 4-6 on page 70 displays homework information for a group of students. (Review homework codes on this page as needed). There are multiple ways this homework chart can be used by individual teachers, parents, teachers and parents who form partnerships and work together, teachers who decide to work with other teachers, persons in charge of after school programs, etc.

- The chart can be used as displayed in example 4-6, enlarged and used as a wall chart or used as a guideline for creating similar charts.

- A teacher may ask each student to use a homework chart like the one presented in example 4-5 to keep track of homework assignments. Each student should also record a homework code at the end of each week. The teacher then holds class competitions to show which group of students did the best job of recording homework completion codes that most accurately reflect homework completion codes recorded on charts maintained by the teacher. The results of the competition is then displayed on wall charts. (Use the fourth suggestion described on page 67 for example 4-4 to set up wall charts.)

EXAMPLE 4-6

Homework Chart: ______________________________
(group of students: grade, section number, etc.)

Names	Oct. 8	Oct. 9	Oct. 10	Oct. 11	Oct. 12	Homework Completion Codes						Homework Completion Codes					
B. Ashford	X	X		X	X	E											
L. Riley		X		/		F											
P. Pollard	X		/		X	G											
J. Harvey		/		/	/	N											

•Homework Chart Activity For An Entire School•

There is another suggestion that I believe is important for a school administrator, team of teachers, etc. to consider. The suggestion is to use a homework chart to implement a competitive school wide homework chart activity. The more uniform student expectations and follow up are throughout a school, the more serious students will be for meeting those expectations. Special rewards can be established for homerooms that perform the best for this activity. Rewards should reflect student interests such as class trips, concerts, etc. This activity can also be implemented by parent groups for their children only, after school and tutorial programs for children involved in these programs, etc. Finding *new ways to think about old strategies* could also result in implementation of the activity for two or more families of children who are cousins, etc. Parents of these children can use the activity to enhance gifts for upcoming holidays, family gatherings, etc.

•Chapter 4 Summary•

Implementing written procedures to monitor children's behavior, tasks, homework, and other activities may seem like a lot of work for parents, teachers, etc. However, it's important that children develop an understanding of the long term effects of their behavior on themselves and others. It's critical that a child, student, etc. identify his/her behavior as being part of an overall pattern of behavior and not just *what I did today or two minutes ago*.

Examples presented in this chapter for a parent to monitor a child in a home may seem like a lot for a parent to implement but, I believe this type of documentation has the potential to decrease a parent's need to be verbal as a child assumes greater responsibility for behaving and completing assigned tasks. Written guidelines can enhance a parent's opportunities to justify a child's allowance money and other rewards. A parent can establish guidelines and rewards over short and increasingly longer periods of time spans. For example, a parent may start by implementing a monitoring plan for short periods of time (two or three days or a week) then gradually increase the time span as a child adapts to the fact that a parent is serious about consistently seeing improvements in a child's behavior, etc. Rewards can be adjusted accordingly.

I don't think I can say it enough, I believe a parent has the greatest opportunity to affect change in a child's behavior. However, a parent may not hesitate to say, *"I don't need all this to control my child."* But the fact is that, in general, children are expected to grow up and, at some point in time, become self-supporting. Therefore, the odds are high that they will encounter many situations (college, work, etc.) that require they follow written guidelines established by others and, they will be monitored accordingly. What better example for a child than to not only be verbally trained by a parent but to be trained by a parent who utilizes written guidelines in the home to ease transition of a child being able to follow written guidelines that are implemented in other environments.

There is another important reason parents should consider implementing a written monitoring plan in homes. Many parents work and are tired when they come home from work. Even if not tired, parents do not always feel like focusing on whether or not their children have thoroughly completed assigned tasks, homework, etc. This may also be the case for stay at home parents. Years ago I worked more hours as a stay at home parent than I ever worked when I taught school. There were many days that I was more than tired by the time my children came home from school. Therefore, it's possible that a written monitoring plan can prove to be very effective by eliminating opportunities for children to take advantage of tired parents. Implementation of a checklist, chart, etc. also has the potential to decrease the need for a parent to be verbally repetitive as well the need to mentally retain detailed information about whether or not a child has completed tasks, homework, etc. over a short or long period of time. Again, this can enhance a parent's decision making for determining appropriate allowances, etc. for a child.

There are many advantages for parents who use charts that include insuring a child doesn't get that *all too common memory lapse* for how assigned tasks should be completed. However, it's important to remember that a parent or designated person should thoroughly describe or demonstrate how tasks should be completed. This can be followed up by having a child write in detail how a task should be completed to verify a child understands what's expected. Another option for follow up is to record a child as he/she describes how a task should be completed. Then a child can play the recorded information back as needed. There are many parents who've had the experience of children telling them that assigned tasks were completed but, they forgot to do this or they forgot to do that. The more a parent moves in the direction of implementing written instructions, etc. for a child completing tasks the less the need to be verbal and the less the opportunity for a child to have memory lapses for completing assigned tasks.

Everything that's described in this book is designed to raise a child's responsibility and accountability for respectfully following directions. A parent's role is such that I will also recommend that a parent discuss, clarify and reinforce for a child how following written guidelines in a home is relevant to following written guidelines establish in schools.

All charts presented in this chapter have multiple uses and can be modified for use by parents, teachers, administrators, etc. It is hoped that this will be the case, that this will be just the beginning of how information, charts, etc. presented in this book will be used. Chapters 7 and 8 contain more examples for how charts are used to monitor academic activities. When we who are in charge become more organized with procedures we establish for kids to follow to get from point A to point Z, kids will become more organized and have greater opportunities to develop necessary skills to be productive members of society when it's their turn to produce.

5

Let's Get Busy! Individual & Partnership Strategies!

The charts described in chapter 4 can be used by people who desire to work individually or form partnerships to improve educational opportunities for students. Chapter 5 reinforces information in chapter 4 by using diagrams to summarize strategies presented in chapter 4 and display additional strategies that can be implemented by individuals or people who form partnerships. Therefore, a person or partners will have options to decide which strategy or strategies they desire to use. A partnership between two or more people, groups, etc. can be initiated by anyone involved in a partnership. For example, a parent can present information to teachers, a parent group, school administrators, churches etc. A teacher can present information to parents, administrators, parent groups, churches, etc. Again, the goal here is to create structured activities and expand opportunities for all who desire to contribute to resolving student behavior issues to improve educational opportunities for kids.

Pages 74-75 display a diagram of strategies for a parent or a teacher. Due to the length of the diagram, strategies for the self-monitoring chart that was presented in chapter 4 on pg.63 are displayed at the end of the diagram for pages 74-75. Diagrams of strategies for people who form partnerships are displayed on pages 76-81. As I previously stated, it is hoped that what's presented in this book will be just the beginning of how information will be used.

•Charts: Strategies For Parents And Strategies For Teachers•

Chart Examples	Parent Strategies	Teacher Strategies
Example 4-1 (Discipline Chart)	·Review exam. 4-1 (pg.59), exam. 4-2 (pg.60) and sample codes pg.62 as needed. Strategy 1 Follow examples 4-1 and 4-2 to prepare and implement a discipline (behavior) chart for a family of children. Strategy 2 Prepare a chart to display weekly progress for completion of tasks, homework, etc. Write column headings/dates that represent what's being monitored. (Column Heading Examples: Homework / May 8-14, Bedroom Tasks / June 12-18, etc.) Select and write a code, symbol, etc. in each child's box that represent how well homework, tasks, etc. are completed for the week. This chart can display a great amount of information. Therefore, it is an excellent 'summary' chart.	·Review example 4-1as needed. Strategy 1 Follow example 4-1 to prepare and implement discipline charts for all classes, groups of students, etc. Strategy 2 Display a chart on a bulletin board that shows weekly progress for student behavior written on discipline charts. Each dated column should represent one week of behavior information that's written on discipline charts that are used daily.
Example 4-2 (Letter/Codes Sheet)	·Optional. Use as desired.	·Review example 4-2 as needed. Strategy If you elect to use the Letter/Codes Sheet that includes codes, add new codes as needed. If you use the Letter/Codes Sheet without codes, create a set of codes. You may also opt to create a set of codes without using either sheet.
Example 4-5 (homework chart/one child)	·Review example 4-5 (pg.68) as needed. Strategy 1 Prepare and implement chart by following example 4-5. Verify homework assignments with a teacher or teachers. Strategy 2 Consider preparing a chart for a child's non-homework class assignments. Follow the homework chart example to prepare the chart. Verify assigned work with a teacher or teachers.	·Optional. Use as desired.

Chart Examples	Parent Strategies	Teacher Strategies
Example 4-6 (homework chart for more than one child)	·Optional. Use as desired or follow the recommended strategy for a teacher.	·Review example 4-6 (pg.70) as needed. Strategy Follow example 4-6 to prepare a chart to display on a bulletin board.
Example 4-3 (self-monitoring chart) Reminder Examples 4-3 & 4-4 utilize the same self-monitoring chart.	·Review example 4-3 (pg.63) as needed. Strategy 1 Write a chart heading for tasks to be completed. (Examples: Bedroom Tasks, Behavior Chart, etc.) Develop a set of codes based on the chart's title. (behavior codes, tasks in one room, tasks throughout the home, etc.) Write code symbols and codes in the wide column on the left side of the chart. Date narrow columns. Write codes as needed in each column. Write a weekly progress code. Strategy 2 Follow strategy 1, but, if simpler, substitute numbers for codes. Strategy 3 (This strategy is suggested if tasks need to be divided up daily, etc.) Prepare chart by assigning one room to clean, several tasks throughout the home, etc. Write codes for all tasks in the wide column on the left side of the chart. Date each narrow column and write codes for one, two or three tasks in each column. Tasks should be circled as they are completed. Write a weekly progress code in the designated area at the top of the chart. Write follow up comments as necessary on back of the chart. Strategy 4 Follow the teacher's strategy # 2 but create a self-monitoring behavior chart for a child's classroom. (one chart per classroom) If a child's teacher has implemented a self-monitoring behavior chart for the class you select, make a duplicate copy of the chart already implemented and keep track of the child's progress. If not, create a set of codes for a class and request the child write codes daily. Follow up by discussing progress with a teacher.	·Review example 4-3 as needed. Strategy 1 Assign this chart for all students. Pass out at the beginning of and collect at the end of each class period. Instruct students to write behavior codes as needed. Remind students that the goal is to eliminate or minimize the need to write behavior codes. Students should review previously documented behavior and strive to improve behavior daily. Strategy 2 Create a self-monitoring assignment for 'home tasks.' Allow each student to develop a set of behavior codes for an area or a room in the student's home that he/she is responsible for cleaning. A student or a parent can write codes for incomplete tasks or completed tasks in dated columns. Homework should be signed by a parent and returned for extra credit, class discussion, etc. Option: Consider allowing each group of students to select one room in a home and create one set of codes for this assignment that will be used by all students.

•Partnership Strategies•

Partnerships presented in this book can be initiated by individuals, institutions, organizations, etc. that desire to collaborate with others to improve educational opportunities for kids. It is hoped that strategies presented here will be utilized and result in *new ways to think about old strategies* that will make a difference for kids everywhere.

<table>
<tr><th>Partnership Initiator</th><th>Strategies
(for partnership initiator and partner/s)</th></tr>
<tr><td>Teacher</td><td><u>Partner/s: Parent/s</u>
➢ Schedule a meeting with a group of parents to introduce them to the discipline plan you've implemented by utilizing information contained in this book. Request that parents consider implementing the plan for parents then partnering with you to discuss follow up strategies that will improve student behavior.

➢ Discuss strategies for ways to share information with a parent or parents who follow the plan in this book for monitoring student behavior, etc. in homes. This can insure that one or more students are aware of and responsive to collaborative efforts between teacher and parent.
Examples:
1. Set up columns on a discipline chart used in the home and classroom to record follow up information obtained from each other.
2. Discuss rewards that can be used for improved student behavior.

➢ Inform parents that you will mail a Letter/Codes Sheet home prior to a card marking period, etc. Discuss follow up strategies, rewards, etc. based on information mailed home.

<u>Partner/s: Teacher/s</u>
➢ Schedule a meeting with one or more teachers to introduce them to and/or discuss the discipline plan you've implemented in the classroom by utilizing information contained in this book. Request that a teacher or teachers partner with you to implement the plan in two or more classrooms. Discuss strategies to share information for the purpose of improving student behavior.

➢ Read and discuss chapter 7, Cooperative Monitoring: Grade Level & School Wide. Work together to set up documentation sheets and share information based on information presented in chapter 7.</td></tr>
</table>

Partnership Initiator (continued)	**Strategies** (for partnership initiator and partner/s) **(continued)**
School Administrator	**<u>Partners: Teachers</u>** ➢ Provide consistent and strong support for teachers who are well organized and willing to work in individual classrooms and work with school staff to consistently implement a structured classroom management plan. ➢ Discuss strategies that will demonstrate a unified effort between administrative and teaching staff to improve student accountability. For example, provide support that's needed as teachers implement assignments for all students in a school. Examples: 1) <u>Homework Charts</u>: Require that all students maintain an individual homework chart. (review Example 4-5; pg.68) Require that teachers maintain monitoring charts for tracking completion of homework assignments. (review Example 4-6; pg.70) Establish school-wide rewards based on activities students enjoy. 2) <u>Self Monitoring Behavior Chart</u>: Require that all students maintain this chart. (review Example 4-3; pg.63) Establish strong consequences for students who don't. Establish rewards for students who maintain the chart and consistently display excellent behavior or show noticeable and consistent improvement in all classrooms and other areas of the school. **<u>Partners: Non-Teaching Staff Persons (school security, teacher's assistant, etc.)</u>** ➢ Set up an in-house detention center that will be monitored by non-teaching staff persons. (Teachers should have the option to monitor the detention center.) 1) <u>In House Detention Center</u>: Students assigned to an in-house detention center will be monitored by following the discipline plan presented in this book. (review pgs.50-60) Set up a large 3-ring folder that will contain a discipline chart for each group of students in the school. (Request that each homeroom teacher prepare a master chart and run copies as needed.) Use behavior codes to document student behavior in the detention center. 2) <u>Materials needed for the center</u>: Several dictionaries, pencils, ink pens, line paper, plain paper, colored pencils, folders. 3) <u>Assignment</u> (one assignment for all students): Set up a folder for each student who is assigned to the detention center. The folder should contain all work that the student completes in the center. Start with the first word in the dictionary. Students will write the word, definition and one or two short paragraphs that describes how the word can be used. Students have the option to draw approved diagrams, pictures, etc. to enhance descriptions. Students should work the entire time they are in the center. Collect assignments and keep in folders. Set up a file cabinet for folders that will be filed in alphabetical order. Access a student's folder each time the student returns to the center. The student will continue where he/she left off in a dictionary.

Partnership Initiator (continued)	Strategies (for partnership initiator and partner/s) (continued)
School Administrator continued	**Partners: Non-Teaching Staff Persons (continued)** 4) Consequence for Unruly Behavior: Students who do not follow established rules should receive automatic suspensions from school, no exceptions. Documentation Sheets (chapter 7) for disruptive students should be established in a centralized location and suspension information should be logged on these sheets. **Partner/s: Parent Group/s** ➢ Schedule meetings with parents to introduce, discuss and collaborate to implement all or elements of the plan presented in this book. Discussions should include reward considerations for students who show improvement based on the plan presented in this book. (Rewards can also be considered for parents of those students.) **Partner/s: Parent Group/s & Teachers** ➢ Schedule meetings with parent groups and teachers to introduce, discuss, collaborate, etc. to implement all or elements of the plan presented in this book. Discussions should emphasize collaboration between parents and teachers to implement the plan presented in this book. There should be strong administrative support for implemented strategies with a strong emphasis on student accountability. **Partner/s: Lunchroom Aides** ➢ Set up a folder that contains discipline charts for each group of students that eat in a lunchroom. Establish rules for students to follow in the lunchroom. If necessary, develop a specific set of behavior codes to document the behavior of rule violators. Use a minimum of two lunchroom aides, one to handle charts and the other to approach students as necessary. When a student violates a rule, the mobile lunchroom aide should signal, approach the student, etc. to go over to the stationary lunchroom aide who will request the student's name and document the behavior. (I suggest using I.D. badges for students.) Establish strong consequences for students who violate rules, give wrong names, etc. If necessary, instruct students to sit alphabetically for easier student identification. Also, do not allow students to talk extremely loud, yell, etc. Establish a form, etc. that can be use to write up lunchroom rule violations that require administrative action. **Partners: All Staff Persons** ➢ Read chapter 7 that describes how to set up student Documentation Sheets to centralize student behavior information for the entire school. This chapter also discusses how to improve student behavior in halls areas which is crucial to setting the tone throughout a school. **Partners: After School And/Or Tutorial Programs** ➢ Administrators should meet with persons in charge of these programs to discuss how these programs can reinforce strategies presented in this book.

Partnership Initiator (continued)	Strategies (for partnership initiator and partner/s) (continued)
School Administrator continued	**<u>Partner: Church/s</u>** ➢ Develop a written plan that describes how volunteers, monetary donations, etc. can be used. (Follow whatever legal guidelines that must be in place to utilize the services of volunteers, monetary donations, etc.) Consider using monetary donations to sponsor trips for students whose behavior is good and students who show noticeable improvement in behavior. Consider including parents in trips. Also consider establishing rewards for families where all children in one family do well behaviorally. This option could be extended to include families of siblings and cousins, etc. ➢ School administrators should insure that a school is well-run and prepared to benefit from monetary donations, volunteer help, etc. Church volunteers should not be exposed to out of control student behavior. ➢ Send school representatives into 3 to 5 churches. Request that each church send volunteers into the school to work with teachers, students, etc. in one department only (<u>examples</u>: math classes only, reading classes only, etc) Request that each volunteer donate minimally ½ day a month to work with a classroom teacher. **<u>Partner/s: Other Organization/s, Company, Etc.</u>** ➢ Contact an organization or company to request volunteer service. <u>Example</u>: Contact an engineering firm and request that one or more representatives from the firm meet with a math teacher, a science teacher, etc. and collaborate to help students develop a class project. Work with representatives to determine the number of follow up visits each representative will make to see a project through. Plan class trips to representatives companies.
Parent	**<u>Partner/s: Parent/s</u>** ➢ Schedule a meeting with a group of parents to introduce them to the discipline plan you've implemented by utilizing information contained in this book. Request that parents consider implementing the plan in their homes. Schedule ongoing meetings to continue discussing and implementing strategies that will improve student behavior. ➢ Request that a school administrator give parents permission to conduct 'assembly style' meetings with their children to discuss and reinforce the fact that parents are working with teachers to improve student behavior. (Teachers may attend or participate in conducting the meeting.) Explain strategies that will be implemented. Examples: 1) Set up one or two columns on discipline charts used in homes and classrooms to record follow up information a teacher shares with a parent and vice versa. 2) Discuss rewards that can be used for improved student behavior. ➢ Discuss follow up strategies that can be implemented by a group of parents for Letter/Codes Sheets that teachers mail home prior to card marking periods.

Partnership Initiator (continued)	**Strategies** (for partnership initiator and partner/s) **(continued)**
Grandparent (not living in home with grandchildren) **<u>Note:</u>** This strategy can be used by other relatives such as a non-custodial parent, aunt, etc.	**<u>Partner/s: Parent/s of Grandchildren & Grandchildren</u>** ➢ There are many grandparents who would like to contribute to helping their grandchildren develop excellent behavior in homes and schools. The following strategy may help accomplish this goal. I will use a grandchild's bedroom to describe the strategy. (review Example 4-3; pg.63; self-monitoring chart) 1) Request that a grandchild make a list of all tasks that must be completed to clean his/her bedroom. The list should be verified by the grandchild's parent who can elect to modify the list as needed. 2) Set up a self-monitoring chart for the bedroom that the grandchild will clean. 3) Make copies of the chart then send the chart by e-mail or mail it to the grandchild or grandchild's parent/s. 4) Request that the chart be completed weekly or bi-weekly, signed by a parent and sent back to you by e-mail, mail, etc. 5) Follow up as desired or needed (discussions, rewards, allowances, etc.). ➢ Consider implementation of this plan with a grandchild's teacher or teachers.
Churches	**<u>Partner: School/s</u>** The ratio of churches to schools can generally be written as an improper fraction that shows, in many cities, there are a tremendous number of churches compared to the number of schools. Therefore, there are generally enough churches such that two or more churches could elect to provide volunteer services, monetary donations, etc. to one school and, if this occurred for all schools in many cities, there would still be churches left over. As a result, I'm suggesting the following strategy that will give a church an opportunity to concentrate on helping a specific group of students in a school. This can maximize how volunteer resources are used and make it easier to follow up on the effectiveness of a church's contribution to helping a school. Therefore I suggest that a church: ➢ Send a church representative to meet with a school leader, principal, etc. 1) Verify that there is order in the school such that poor student behavior is not an issue. 2) Provide volunteers, monetary donations, etc. to help students in one department only (example: math, science, etc.). 3) Request a written plan that details how volunteers, monetary contributions, etc. will be used. The plan should include evaluation forms that can be completed by any or all adults who are involved in or benefit from contributions made by a church. 4) Request that each volunteer donate a minimum of 3 hours one day a month to work with a teacher and students in a classroom. (Several volunteers can be assigned to one classroom if enough are available. A teacher should include a written plan for how volunteers will be used in the detailed plan presented to churches.) 5) Brainstorm to improve and/or develop additional strategies to enhance this process.

Partnership Initiator (continued)	Strategies (for partnership initiator and partner/s) (continued)
Churches continued	**Partners: Parents** ➢ Establish parent groups within the church that will meet for the purpose of improving parenting skills to manage the behavior of children. ➢ Provide this book as a resource material for parent workshops, meeting, etc. ➢ Discuss strategies for implementation of the plan described in this book for homes and schools.
Other Organization, Firm, Company, Etc.	**Partners: Schools** ➢ Meet with school leaders to establish schedules for representatives of organizations, firms, etc. to work with teachers to implement specific lessons, class projects, etc. that connect real life experiences with concepts presented in textbooks. ➢ Follow strategies described for churches.

PART II

Classroom Management: Monitoring In Action!

Part II Overview

Part II focuses on how O. Hemphill's original classroom management plan was implemented. Information presented in part II continues to be relevant for what needs to be done to resolve student behavior problems for the purpose of improving educational opportunities for kids. However, this section also contains updated information based on O. Hemphill's consultant experiences since retiring in 2001. For example, chapter 8 contains several examples of how O. Hemphill used charts to monitor academic activities and these examples include updated information. Although there is a great deal of emphasis on what happens with classroom teachers, parents and other people outside the teaching profession can develop tremendous understanding of how classroom management strategies can be implemented by reading this section. The more knowledgeable non-teaching persons are about how classroom management strategies are implemented the greater the opportunity to effectively contribute to helping improve educational opportunities for students.

Chapter 6 Overview: Showtime: Classroom Monitoring In Action!

- This chapter uses real life classroom experiences as examples to demonstrate classroom management strategies that are presented in this book.

Chapter 7 Overview: Cooperative Monitoring: Grade Level & School Wide

- This chapter describes how Documentation Sheets and Discipline Charts can be used to implement cooperative monitoring activities in individual classrooms and/or throughout a school.

Chapter 8 Overview: Monitoring Academic And Random Activities

- This chapter shows several examples of how charts are used to monitor academic activities. These examples clearly reinforce the fact that a teacher can move in the direction of becoming more of a facilitator and less of a lecturer when implementing academic activities.

6

Showtime: Classroom Monitoring In Action!

There are many strategies that can be used to minimize the work involved in implementing a discipline chart. Strategies include doing the opposite of what's expected. For example, when I taught school there were incidents where disruptive students outnumbered good students. One of my favorite strategies was to quickly document this type of disruption by dating a column on a discipline chart and writing a check mark (√) in the dated column next to the name of each student who was not involved in the disruption. I would date the back of a discipline chart, write a check mark in parenthesis (√) and write one or two statements that described the incident and clarified that a check mark was placed in boxes of students who were not disruptive. When a class settled down I explained what I did. Later, when time allowed, I would write a code for the incident in boxes of disruptive students and write an additional statement on back of the discipline chart to clarify that the code identified behavior for these students. This strategy proved to be effective until I retired.

Doing the opposite of what's expected can also be effective when disruptive behavior occurs and a disruption is not documented. For example, I resolved several disruptive outbursts that occurred during my teaching years by saying nothing as I gave students a *firm look* until they quieted down. Then I'd ask a question such as the following. *"Is there someone here who's deaf and can't hear?"* Students usually looked puzzled but would remain quiet. Then I'd make comments such as the following. *"Oh! I didn't think so. I'm trying to understand why several of you are yelling like you're trying to talk to someone in another classroom."* Disruptive students would quickly realize their attempt to unnerve me by displaying disruptive behavior had failed. My ability to respond to disruptions by staying calm but firmly looking at students as I said nothing was all it took many times to stop disruptive behavior and it minimized the potential for me to make mistakes when attempting to identify disruptive students.

There's nothing quite like doing the unexpected to capture the attention of disruptive students. There's a feeling of empowerment when you realize that it doesn't require yelling, etc. to resolve disruptive student behavior incidents. Now let's take a look at other examples of how I used discipline charts in classrooms. In other words, *let's continue to take a walk in my shoes.*

•A New School Year Or A New Group Of Students•

Student behavior has deteriorated to the extent that a teacher must be prepared to handle unruly students the first day the teacher encounters students. There was a time when a teacher had the opportunity to introduce him/her self with pleasant greetings and a discussion of wonderful planned activities for the year. Unfortunately, in too many classrooms, this is no longer the case as too many students enter classrooms with the intent to display disruptive behavior before a teacher even gets the opportunity to say hello, good morning, etc. I can't say it enough, it's critical that a teacher has a classroom management plan in place to insure students quickly understand who's *running the show* in a classroom.

An important component of a good classroom management plan is a quick and accurate procedure for identifying and documenting the behavior of unruly students. The following description represents a *'first day of school experience'* that occurred during the years I taught school. Again, this experience reflects a pattern of unruly student behavior that's all too common when a teacher encounters a new group of students.

On the first day of school I allowed students to enter the classroom without giving them any instructions about where to sit or how to behave. (However, students were informed to stay seated after selecting seats.) I wanted to see how they handled themselves without my input. There were rare occasions when a school year started with students displaying appropriate behavior as they entered the classroom. Unfortunately, today was not one of those rare occasions. Several students entered the classroom, sat down and talked as if they were trying to be heard by students in another school. When this occurred I followed my plan and observed students without talking as I passed out attendance cards for completion. I looked directly at several unruly students as I scanned the room. I was slightly amused at the fact unruly students saw me watching them and, when I didn't say anything, continued talking. During the scanning I 'locked in' on two or three students I wanted to identify and document behaviorally. I used line paper and wrote seat number locations for these students. Then I wrote a brief description of their behavior. The information would be transferred to a temporary or permanent discipline chart as soon as I obtained their names. (Review chapter 4 as needed for discipline chart information.) When I collected attendance cards, I wrote seat numbers on cards of students selected for documentation. Next, I replaced seat numbers written on line paper with names of selected students.

When I was ready to talk to the group I stood with good posture similar to soldiers during drill practice. I didn't talk as I continued scanning the room and waiting for students to quiet down without my help. Students continued talking so I sat down, waited approximately one minute then stood up again. By this time several students were trying to figure out why I hadn't said anything. They started quieting down without my help. I observed some students telling others to be quiet as I continued waiting. When students finally quieted down I said, "I'm happy to see you realize you should quiet down without my help. I'm concerned that several of you talked without my permission, particularly that you talked as loud as you did. I thank those of you who entered the classroom in a respectful manner, found a seat, sat down and were quiet as you waited for me to greet the class." I stopped talking and looked directly at students I previously identified. Then I informed the entire class that students should pay attention to what I'd do when disruptions occurred. They would see that I'd be quiet and observant during disruptions to insure I could accurately identify and describe the behavior of as many unruly students as possible.

I continued the discussion by talking about the discipline chart I'd use to monitor students behaviorally. By now several students were quiet and not too thrilled their first day behavior routine had been modified. I completed the discussion by describing behavior of documented students and informed these students that documented information would be transferred to a temporary discipline chart until I made the decision as to whether or not it would be transferred to a permanent discipline chart. I observed 'sighs of relief' as documented students realized they might be given a second chance to redeem themselves. It was apparent that my goal had been accomplished and students understood I had a plan for identifying and documenting unruly students even when I said nothing to stop the behavior. I felt like a basketball player who had just scored the winning points in a final playoff game to secure a championship for a basketball team.

First day student identification and monitoring can be made easier by using a class list to prepare a seating and a discipline chart before students enter a classroom. A letter/codes sheet should also be available for immediate use (review Chapter 4; pg.60). If students are not sitting in assigned seats when a disruption occurs, the procedure described in the *'first day of school experience'* on pages 84-85 can be used to resolve the problem. If students are sitting in assigned seats and a behavior problem occurs, stay calm and look firm as you focus on as many disruptive students as possible. (This may only be one or two students.) Use a letter/codes sheet to select behavior codes, date a column on a discipline chart and document unruly behavior in appropriate student boxes. If several students are involved in displaying the same disruptive behavior (loud talking, yelling, etc), as I stated at the beginning of this chapter, a check mark (√) can be written in boxes of respectful students to expedite recording the behavior and an explanation written on back of the chart.

If a class list is not available, another strategy for handling disruptive behavior is to pass out attendance cards for students to complete. Use a copy of the 8½ in. x 11in. grid in the supplement to set up a temporary discipline chart. On the temporary discipline chart write seat number locations in the column where students' names are written until names of unruly students can be obtained from attendance cards. Use behavior codes on a letter/codes sheet to document unruly behavior on a temporary discipline chart. Again, check marks can also be used to expedite documentation if several students display the same unruly behavior. Use a pencil to prepare a seating chart as quickly as possible after collecting attendance cards. (I alphabetized cards while students were in the classroom the first day.) After completing a seating chart, have students move as quickly as possible to assigned seats. In my classroom I read names and seat assignments then ask students to move to assigned seats. This gave me another opportunity to identify unruly students. I will also say that the fact that I was as serious as I was about students behaving usually resulted in minimal seat changes after I wrote a seating chart. I'm sure you've noticed that I haven't referred to a seating chart as 'a temporary seating chart.' Well, I really didn't buy into a statement that is fairly common for students to say to teachers. The statement: *"I can't sit next to him/her because we don't get along."* My response in general was, *"You're responsible for being okay in the seat I assign you. If there's a problem, respectfully address it to me so it can be resolved in a reasonable manner."* Therefore, temporary seating charts I wrote weren't far removed from permanent seating charts that were established. Example 6-1 below shows a seating arrangement I used for several years.

EXAMPLE 6-1

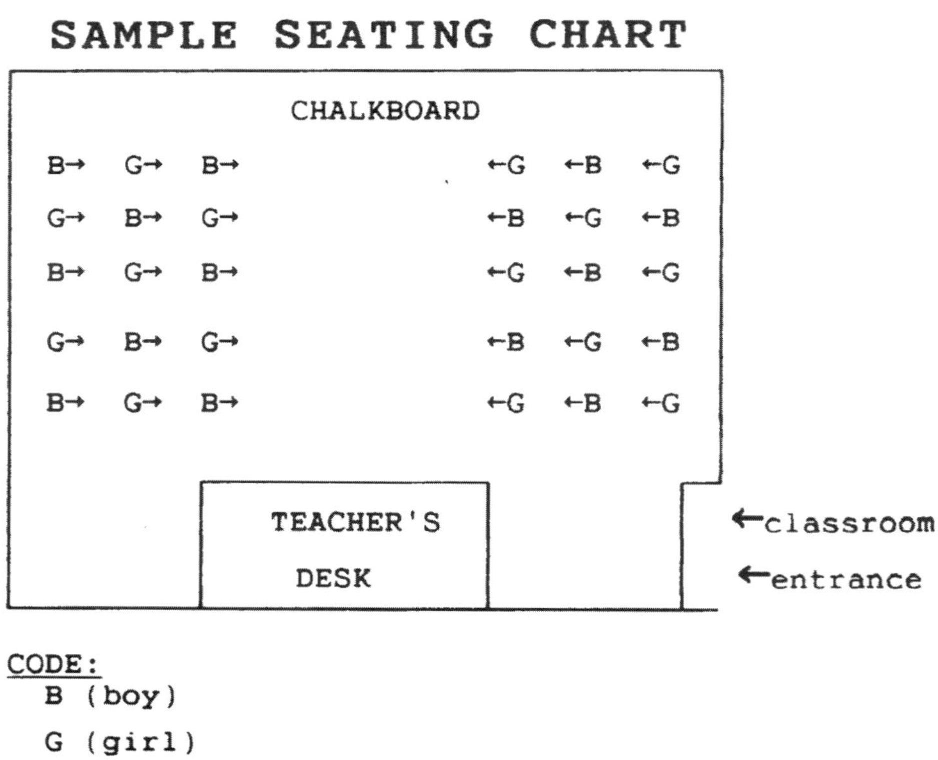

The seating chart arrangement in example 6-1 opened up the classroom and made it easier for me to be in close proximity to all students. This was an important factor for being able to manage students behaviorally and most certainly made a difference the first time I encountered a group of students. Again, as previously described, I made it a priority to document the behavior of two or three students who displayed unruly behavior on the first day of a new school year. I'm a firm believer that unruly students *bring the behavior into* a *classroom*. Therefore, teachers must be proactive and prepare to identify and document behavior of unruly students soon after they enter a classroom. However, it's important to know that if you are a teacher in a situation where several students display disruptive behavior at the same time, you should not be concerned if you can't identify all disruptive students at one time. What's important is that students quickly understand that you have a procedure for identifying and documenting as many unruly students as you can the first day of school or the first day you encounter a new group of students. Students who continue to display disruptive behavior will have their turn to be documented. Believe it!

Information written on a temporary discipline chart can be used to enhance the explanation of a permanent discipline chart. If extreme behavior occurs, you should consider transferring documented information from a temporary discipline chart onto a permanent discipline chart. Before students enter classrooms they are aware of specific disruptive behaviors that should not occur. They should immediately be held accountable for not displaying these behaviors.

As previously stated, if disruptive behavior occurs the first day of school and time allows, it may be necessary to give a brief explanation of the discipline chart that will be used to monitor unruly students. Use this book and refer to Examples 4-1 and 4-2, pgs.59 and 60 as you explain a discipline chart and letter/codes sheet. Inform students that you are implementing a classroom management plan that is similar to a road map and they will be given clear and detailed instructions on how to follow it. I suggest that you walk around the room and use this book to display examples 4-1 and 4-2 as you discuss the effectiveness of a discipline chart. I actually made several copies of the letter/codes sheet and gave students an opportunity to examine it as I discussed how a discipline chart would be used to monitor student behavior. I used the behavior of students who displayed unruly behavior during my first encounter with a group of students to enhance the discussion on how a discipline chart would be implemented. Then I collected letter/codes sheets at the end of a class period.

Some unruly students who are documented will immediately voice complaints that they were not the only students who were disruptive when a disruptive behavior incident occurred. The complaint usually results from the fact that all students who were involved in an incident were not documented. If this happens it's important to remind students that you are only one human being. Tell them it's unfair to place you in a predicament where you must be selective about who will be documented. Clarify that it's their responsibility to make sure they're not included in the group of students displaying unruly behavior.

It is important to insure that students be given opportunities throughout a school year to discuss and ask questions about the classroom management plan that's being implemented, particularly implementation of a discipline chart. This is as important as any lesson you'll ever teach. In fact, I believe it's the first lesson that should be taught before any effort is made to teach academic work. Remember, effective teaching will not occur if students fail to understand or adhere to behavioral expectations. You must be consistent with implementation of a classroom management plan, particularly if you are using a discipline chart to monitor behavior. Students will observe you to verify whether or not you are consistent with what you expect from them behaviorally. From time to time remind students how fast and effective it is to use a discipline chart to monitor student behavior incidents.

Clarify that you will not always monitor unruly behavior by speaking to applicable students. Hold students accountable by explaining that sometimes, if you look directly at select students when unruly behavior occurs, *"they did it!"* Assure students you will discuss whatever is written on the chart at appropriate times when it doesn't interfere with class activities. However, when it's necessary to interrupt the class to make a point, do it but be as calm and brief as possible. It's also important that you clarify that unruly behavior means to violate any rules that have been established for students. This includes something as simple as *chewing gum.*

A discipline chart and letter/codes sheet should be readily available at all times. I suggest using a class folder that can hold all charts that will be used to monitor several activities for a group of students. Students will quickly realize that you are serious about managing a structured classroom. They will quickly familiarize themselves with a set of behavior codes on a letter/codes sheet, etc. I had the experience of being corrected more than once when I mistakenly selected an incorrect behavior code. Students enjoyed opportunities they had to correct me. This can prove to be a nice *bonus for teachers* who from time to time may make mistakes when attempting to identify students who display unruly behavior. *I'm testifying here!*

•Classroom Rules And Student Captains•

Beginning of the year activities should include an explanation of classroom rules. Following is a list of rules used in my classroom.

1. Enter the room quietly.
2. Go directly to your assigned seat and sit down.
3. Do not walk, talk, chew any item, etc. without permission of the teacher or adult in charge.
4. Clear your desk of everything except teacher approved materials. Be prepared to receive instruction when the tardy bell rings.
5. Follow **all** school rules established for students.

Students were responsible for following all rules. They were given a supply list and documented behaviorally for entering the classroom without supplies. I rarely ever *loaned* supplies. A common complaint of a student who was unprepared for instruction was, *"How do you expect me to do the work?"* I usually responded with, *"I expect you to do what respectful students do, bring supplies to class so you have what you need to work."* If I loaned supplies I used M1, M2 or M3 behavior codes to document a student the first time they entered class with missing supplies. (review a letter/codes sheet; pg.60) If a student repeated the behavior he/she was documented for blatant insubordination. I would write the appropriate code/s in the student's box and write the word **"over"** to show information was written on back of the chart. Then I dated the back of the chart, wrote the student's name and a brief explanation of the problem. This usually resolved the problem because students didn't like to be documented for blatant insubordination because they didn't bring supplies to class. If blatant insubordination is considered too strong a consequence, I must remind you that you must *'keep your eyes on the prize.'* The prize is a *respectful student* who follows rules with little or no help from you. Never disrespect students who follow rules by allowing unruly students to *get away with* violating rules.

A selection of student captains will also enhance classroom activities. I wanted students to actively participate in making a contribution to a smooth running classroom. Therefore, the following *captains'* positions were established.

- Room captain: a student who examines the classroom near the end of the class period to insure student desks are in correct positions and the floor clear of debris / when the dismissal bell rang the room captain selects rows for dismissal (based on their readiness)

- Front line captain: a student placed in front of the line when students travel though the hall area to another destination and/or back to the classroom

- Back line captain: a student placed in back of the line when students travel through the hall area to another destination and/or back to the classroom

- Paper or pencil captain: a student who passes out or collects paper, pencils, worksheets, etc.

- Book captain/s: a student or students who pass out and collect books (this position should be used at the beginning of the school year until students are assigned textbooks for class and home use

Captains' positions were created as needed. My students were informed captains had to display exemplary behavior. Students who were not selected as captains understood they had to respect the role of captains. They could not interfere with captains' duties without consequences. New captains were chosen monthly. I kept a good record of captains to insure all students had an opportunity to participate during a school year.

•Beginning And Ending Class Sessions•

The way a group of students exit a classroom as a second group enters for instruction determines how much time is wasted settling entering students at the beginning of a class period. As a teacher you must never forget how important this is to set the tone in a classroom. I believe this one factor can make or break your teaching career. All students should be given directions on how to exit and enter a classroom. Entering students should also be given directions on a *direct route* to take to walk to their assigned seats.

The way students enter a classroom is directly related to their behavior in the hall area. Therefore, teachers should perform hall duty to insure a smooth traffic flow as students enter (or exit) classrooms.

I performed hall duty to insure students followed my instructions for entering and exiting the classroom. Hall duty is an important function for administrative and teaching staff because it's one of the few times students have the opportunity to see staff working together as a team. The *tone* of the hall area also provides information about whether or not administrators and teachers are *in charge* of a school. There were wonderful years when I worked with co-workers to perform this duty. It made the job that much easier. However, my commitment to performing hall duty was not based on whether or not other staff persons did the same. Again, I knew this was an important component of effective classroom management and never failed to perform it.

When a dismissal bell rang I picked up an ink pen and class folders containing discipline charts for both groups of students who were exiting and entering the classroom. Discipline charts were placed on top of the folders for quick access in case I spotted behavior problems with students. Exiting students understood they had to be dismissed by the room captain. All students were given directions on how to enter or exit the classroom and walk in the hall area. I stood in the middle of the hall facing the open door to the classroom. I acted as an intersection as students traveled in and out of the classroom. I also observed both groups as they walked in the hall area.

The diagram on page 96 shows directions that were given to students. Students walking towards the classroom on the side of the hall that I was facing turned right to enter the classroom when they reached the door. If they approached the classroom from the opposite side of the hall area to my left, they walked around me (behind my back) to merge with students who entered the classroom by making a right turn. They could not cross in front of me to enter the room. If the exiting class was running late, students entering were instructed to quietly line up near the door. (to my right) They were not allowed to block the door area. Students exiting the classroom were instructed to turn right or cross the hall to my left to insure they traveled on the correct side of the hall.

Did I make a big deal out of students entering and exiting the classroom? You bet I did! It was that important. Again, I also gave students instructions on a *direct route* to take to get to assigned seats. I did not tolerate a student walking to row 3 and then walking to row 5 if the student was assigned to a seat in row 5.

Any inappropriate behavior observed was documented as I performed hall duty. I usually walked in and out of the classroom at least twice while on hall duty to insure students were seated and preparing for instruction. Students had to place assigned supplies on top of their desk and start a bell work assignment that was written on the board.

When the tardy bell rang I entered the classroom, closed the door and greeted students. (*example:* *"Good morning 8-4's or good afternoon 8-4's*) I then scanned the classroom to insure students were following rules, particularly rule # 4 that reads:

> *Clear your desk of everything except teacher approved materials.*
> *Be prepared to receive instruction when the tardy bell rings.*

I did not interrupt the class to name documented students unless I wanted to stress a point. If I observed students who were unprepared for instruction I dated a column on the discipline chart and wrote R4 in applicable student boxes. R4 meant classroom rule # 4 was violated. Students knew who was documented by the way I looked directly at selected students. This improved student accountability for being prepared for instruction when I entered the classroom after the tardy bell rang.

•Tardy Students•

Tardy students should not be allowed to interrupt a class session. There should be a designated area where tardy students can stand until they can be seated. The area should be near the door but not directly in front of the class. Clarify for all students this procedure is not a punishment. The purpose is to insure students entering on time receive uninterrupted instruction. Reiterate for tardy students they will be seated as quickly as possible. They must stand quietly to avoid being documented for distracting behavior. They are also responsible for completing missed work and can request help only to the extent it doesn't require re-teaching a lesson or interfering with students who entered on time. Again, was I serious? Absolutely! The tardy procedure served three purposes.

1. It was easier to identify tardy students.
2. It maximized uninterrupted instruction time for a class.
3. It minimized the number of students who entered late.

Most tardy students didn't want to stand while other students received instruction. It's difficult to write standing up. Tardy students wanted the same opportunity to receive instruction as students who entered on time.

The tardy procedure worked extremely well and was enhanced by following school policy for reporting tardy students to administration. It minimized the number of students I had to refer to an administrator for excessive tardiness because students made a better effort to get to class on time. When students were late, they stood quietly until I signaled them to be seated. They understood unruly behavior would *absolutely* not be tolerated.

If tardy students display unruly behavior while waiting to be seated, do not ignore the importance of documenting the behavior. Remember, you must set the tone for the class session. As you familiarize yourself with charting behavior, you will be able to avoid interrupting class sessions and delay documentation until the class is quietly working. However, if necessary, document immediately for tardy students who display extreme behavior and *send them out of the room as quickly as possible.* It may be necessary to write a pass that includes a brief explanation such as *"The student entered late displaying disruptive behavior. Detailed information will be forthcoming."* If the student leaves the room without a pass, document the behavior as truancy and send information to an administrator as soon as possible. However, do not deprive other students of important instruction time to perform this task.

Behavior codes for tardy students

DE-----disruptive entrance (entering loud or noisy)
DT-----disruptive talking (talking while waiting to be seated)
DN-----disruptive noise (any other noises while waiting to be seated)
Di------distracting students (distracting other students while waiting to be seated)

•A Class Session In Progress•

If inappropriate behavior occurs during a class session, walk towards or pick up the folder containing the discipline chart and letter/codes sheet. Many times this will be enough to stop the behavior. If the behavior stops, decide if documentation is necessary. It's not important to document every problem. It's important to establish a behavior pattern for students who continually display inappropriate behavior.

If inappropriate behavior continues decide if it's necessary to speak to the student or students involved. Remember to remain calm and not raise your voice. It's the responsibility of students to hear you. Pick up the discipline chart and, if possible, document students in order of *worst to least culprit*. Students will usually settle down as they observe you documenting behavior. If a disruptive student or students display anger by yelling out or talking loud, look directly at the student or students and say, *"Are you blurting out?"* or *"Are you talking without my permission?"* Remember to respond as much as possible with comments that reference the behavior. Then, as quickly as possible, direct all students back to completing assigned work.

When appropriate, take the student or students who displayed disruptive behavior to a private area in the room or outside the classroom to discuss the disruption. If a student's behavior results in sending the student from the room, write a note stating documentation will follow later. However, if you must stop a lesson in progress to write a referral, apologize to the class for the interruption and assure students you are doing what's necessary to minimize future disruptions by the same student/s.

There may be times when documenting unruly students will try your patience. However, be consistent! The more consistently you document inappropriate behavior the less you'll observe unruly behavior. Much of what you document can be done while students are quietly working.

The time will arrive when you can document most inappropriate behavior near the end of a class session. I documented most behavior while the room captain was in the process of getting students ready for dismissal. However, document when necessary. Do not attempt to memorize details. You do not want to place yourself in a *'he said, she said'* predicament when talking with administrators or parents about a student's behavior.

From time to time remember to thank students who display exemplary behavior. Respectful students should always know you are aware of their excellent behavior when other students display inappropriate behavior. When disruptions occur, use the behavior of respectful students as a resource to guide your actions. Remember to stay calm as you resolve the disruption. Responding in an angry manner is detrimental to your health and the well being of respectful students. I don't think your body can tolerate twenty-five to thirty years of angry reactions. It's also not fair for respectful students to be subjected to negative behavior displayed by a teacher. You must remember to be an example for all students, even in the worst circumstances.

•Monitoring Student Behavior In Hall Areas•

Students' traveling in the hall area is one of the most important *activities* that occur in schools. There continues to be too many schools where this activity doesn't get the attention it deserves. The way students travel in hall areas is directly related to the way they *behave* in halls and classrooms. Again, student behavior in the hall area reflects the *tone* of a school and determines the degree of effort teachers must use to *settle* students after they enter classrooms.

Teachers' duties usually include escorting students to lunch and school assemblies. Teachers must also escort students out a building during fire drills. The way a teacher handles this duty can reflect whether or not he/she has good classroom management skills. It gives administrators, teachers and students an opportunity to see a teacher's classroom management skills *in action.*

Student travel in hall areas should be orderly. Students should not be allowed to walk in a chaotic manner, run, talk loud or yell, shove each other, etc. without consequences. I implemented a *travel plan* by using front and back line captains whenever I had to escort students in the hall area. The class was given instructions to line up single file between both captains. As much as possible the room captain was given the opportunity to select students to line up for exiting the room. I carried the class folder containing the discipline chart and letter/ codes sheet. Once students were lined up in the hall area I positioned myself near the middle of the line and directed the front line captain to stop at strategic points as the class moved through the hall. When necessary to turn a corner the front line captain was instructed to stop at the end of the hall and wait for me to reach that point. The class then walked around the corner as I observed the entire line. All students understood their responsibility to display appropriate behavior as the class was escorted to and from the classroom. They understood the importance of front and back line captain positions and knew there were consequences for jeopardizing the duties of students assigned to these positions. If it was necessary for me to return to a lunchroom, etc. to escort students back to the classroom, students were instructed on how and where to line up between line captains. If any behavior problems occurred during the time students were escorted to and from the classroom, I documented behavior on the discipline chart as I escorted students or immediately after returning to the classroom.

During fire drills it's critical that students behave in an orderly manner in the hall area. Utilizing front and back line captains makes it easier to know who should be at the front and back of the line. Other students can be held directly accountable for not being in line between line captains as the group exits and reenters the classroom. Students should be given directions on where to stand outside the building as line captains maintain their positions. However, the positions may be reversed when students reenter the building after the drill ends.

Implementation of a *hall area routing plan* is a powerful tool for eliminating problems that occur daily when students travel in the hall area. Following is a partial list of problems common to schools that have no plan or ineffective plans for student behavior and travel in halls.

1. loud talk, yelling, arguing with staff or other students, use of profanity, etc.
2. running, shoving other students, fighting, etc.
3. excessive tardies, skipping classes, etc.

Several years ago I was given the opportunity to discuss my classroom management procedure with teaching and administrative staff after being observed in the classroom and observed escorting students in the hall area. This eventually resulted in my developing a plan for routing all students in the building. The plan was accepted and implemented by administrative and teaching staff. It improved the overall tone of the school. In 1990 I was nominated by my peers to compete for a *Teacher Of The Year Award* being offered by Detroit Board of Education. I was one of fourteen Detroit teachers selected to receive the award that was presented during a ceremony at Cobo Hall in Detroit, Michigan. To this day I consider this to be one of my greatest accomplishments because I was selected by my peers.

One of the most common solutions implemented to resolve the *hall area dilemma* is *hall sweeps*. Are they a waste of time or what? I'm just keeping it real. As far as I'm concerned, hall sweeps imply large numbers of students will not be expected to follow rules established for eliminating truancy in hall areas. The problem is made worse as students run and suddenly bang on classroom doors in an attempt to avoid being caught during hall sweeps. Hall sweeps do not help students understand their responsibility to enter classrooms in a timely fashion and they certainly don't help students understand administration is serious about implementing consequences for students who are late to or truant from classes.

More practical solutions are readily available for administrative and teaching staffs that work together to develop and implement plans for resolving the *hall area dilemma*. However, I don't believe the problem is lack of solutions. I believe the problem stems from failure to understand the magnitude of the effect poor student behavior in hall areas has on efforts to educate students. The result is failure to consistently implement plans that have been established to eradicate poor student behavior in hall areas. Therefore, students pay little or no attention to discipline plans established to insure students display appropriate behavior in hall areas.

I can't say the following statement enough. I strongly believe that, *students' behavior in hall areas reflect the tone of a school*. It also affects the degree of *tiredness* administrative, teaching staff and other staff persons experience by the end of a school day. I had many wonderful days where I ended the day feeling tired due to *noise level* in the hall area. I also sympathized with lunch staff that was exposed on a daily basis to students yelling an entire lunch hour. Years of noisy halls, lunchrooms, assemblies, etc. can take a physical and emotional toll on school staff. Implementing effective student behavior plans to insure students display appropriate behavior in hall areas will be a tremendous step towards retaining good teaching staff, etc. in applicable schools I will reiterate the importance of resolving this dilemma by reminding you that time wasted in classrooms usually start with how students enter and /or exit classrooms and, guess what, *they usually enter classrooms from hall areas*.

Hall area behavior codes

DW-----disruptive walking
DT------disruptive talking
DL------disruptive laughing
DP------disruptive playing
Sh-------shoving a student or students
R--------running

EXAMPLE 6-2

The following diagram shows how students should enter the classroom.

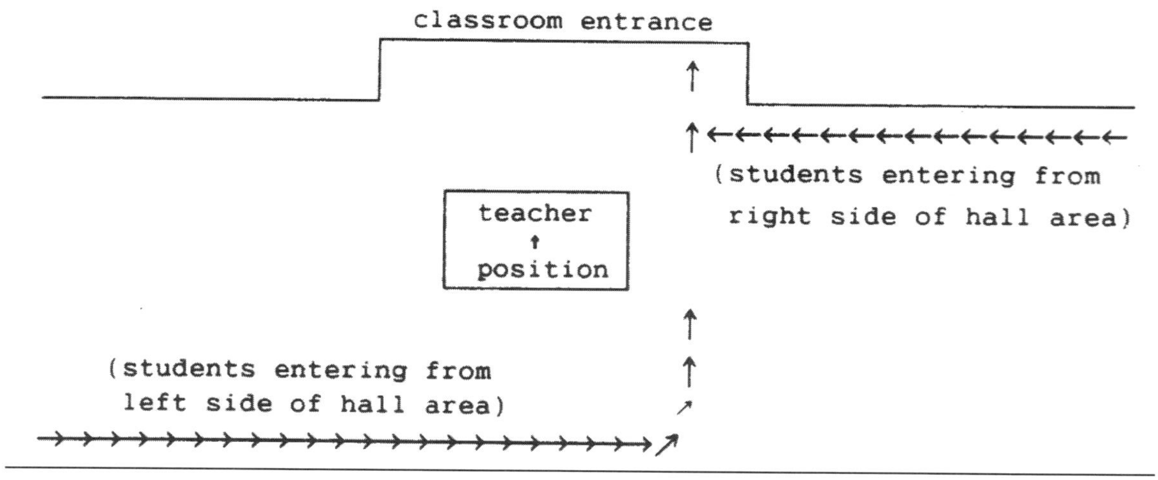

EXAMPLE 6-3

The following diagram shows how students should exit the classroom.

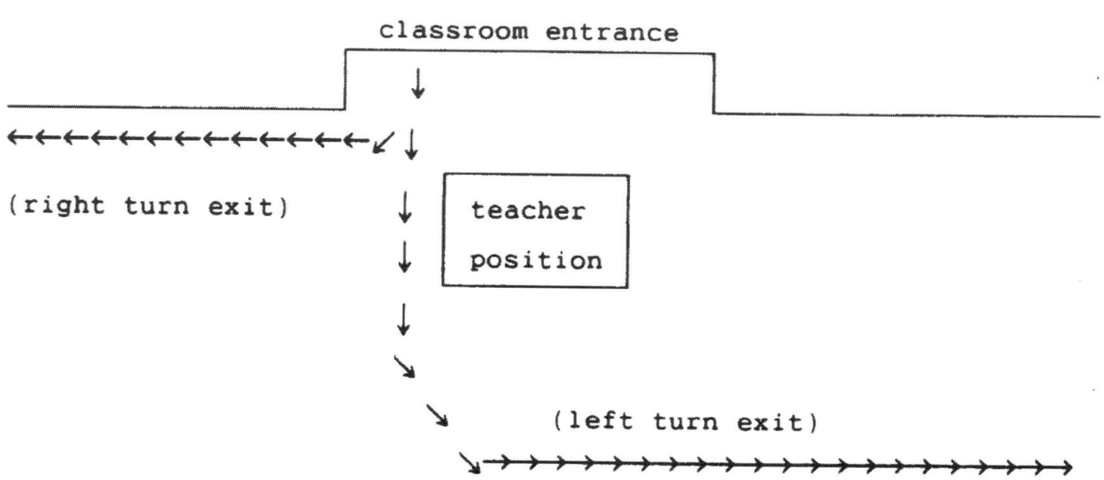

•Fights•

Fighting is intolerable behavior that should be resolved before it ever occurs. Students should be given instructions on what to do if a fight breaks out. I decided years ago to prioritize the steps I'd take to resolve fights. The following steps were explained to students so they clearly understood what I believe a teacher should or shouldn't do to handle this incident. I was fortunate to have only one fight in the classroom during my teaching years. Fortunately, by the time it occurred, I remembered the following steps that I explained to all classes I taught and I did a magnificent job implementing them.

1. You (the teacher) must protect yourself and stay in charge of *all* students. Remain calm and say to fighting students, *"Stop fighting."* Do not yell. Remember, students are responsible for hearing you. You must not distract or incite other students by yelling.

2. Protect other students. There should be a designated area for students to move to as soon as a fight starts. My students were instructed to quickly and quietly line up by lockers in the hall area and remain quiet.

3. Do not allow other students to *fuel the fight* without consequences. If this happens document as many unruly students as possible. Clarify the behavior will be considered dangerous and will be treated as seriously as the behavior of fighting students.

4. Seek administrative help or help from a security staff person.

5. Send or have fighting students escorted to an administrator. If previous behavior problems have been documented on fighting students, follow up written referrals by sharing previously documented information with an administrator.

During my teaching career there were two major incidents in my classroom where students jumped up to fight. I can quickly summarize incident number one as *"We thought we wanted to fight but when Ms. Hemphill gave us 'the look' we changed our minds and sat down."* That's exactly how the first incident occurred.

Incident number two (previously described0 was an actual fight between two girls. It was later discovered that an argument had been *brewing* for several days between the girls. On the day of the fight the class was quietly working on an assignment when both girls suddenly leaped from their seats and started fighting each other. I was stunned and angered by the behavior but responded calmly and followed the procedure I established for handling a fight. I said, *"Stop fighting."* Then, I escorted other students to a safe area outside the classroom and pressed a button on the intercom system to summon security. I stood near the door where I could watch the class and students who were fighting. I waited patiently until the girls got tired and stopped fighting. I did not allow other students to break up the fight. When security came, I gave the girls an opportunity to straighten up the room before being escorted out and suspended for several days. They were remorseful. They apologized and accepted the opportunity.

During a conference with parents of the girls who fought I explained the procedure established for handling fights in my classroom. I clarified the classroom environment was peaceful when the girls suddenly jumped up and started fighting. The parents weren't *thrilled* that I didn't physically attempt to stop the fight. However, they couldn't argue with the following facts.

1. I always conducted an organized and well-managed classroom that was conducive to learning.

2. I protected myself and other students from being injured and did not tolerate other students fueling the fight.

3. Fighting students were responsible for fighting and should have willingly sought help from an adult to resolve the problem prior to fighting.

Every strategy utilized was designed to insure students assumed responsibility for their behavior. I had no problem sharing this information with parents.

•Monitoring Reminders•

Effective monitoring of unruly students requires that you (the teacher) train yourself to consistently implement a monitoring procedure. You must consistently document poor student behavior to insure students understand you are serious about behavioral expectations. If necessary, the behavior should be documented when it occurs to avoid trying to remember details later. Otherwise, document as soon as possible without interrupting or distracting other students from class activities.

Make a determination as inappropriate behavior occurs about whether or not it needs documentation. I documented as much as possible early in the school year to settle students and minimize the amount of inappropriate behavior displayed by students as the school year continued. As I stated in a previous chapter, documentation on a discipline chart serves the purpose of establishing patterns of behavior for unruly students. Therefore, it's not necessary to document every single problem that occurs. It's a judgment call that you must make. However, the more students realize you are documenting behavior, particularly behavior such as gum chewing, whispering, etc., the better they'll behave.

Be strategic about referring students to administrators. I generally referred students for continuous or extreme unruly behavior. When I wrote a referral it contained several dates of behavioral information. The more consistent you are with documentation, the less you'll write referrals or feel the need to respond in an angry manner when problems occur. There should never under any circumstances be an *out of control* verbal exchange between you and an unruly student. Too many teachers have been rated unsatisfactory as a result of displaying out of control behavior and/or not implementing an effective classroom management system. Do not allow yourself to become a member of this group. Review the following monitoring reminders as often as needed to stay on top of *your game*.

1. Establish a monitoring system to monitor inappropriate student behavior.
2. Begin explaining behavioral expectations and the monitoring system to students the first week of school. Provide opportunities for students to discuss and ask questions to clarify behavioral expectations, consequences, etc.
3. Be consistent with documenting behavior.
4. Use responses that refer to rules violated when talking to students who display inappropriate behavior. (example: *"I don't remember giving you permission to walk to the pencil sharpener."*)
5. Perform hall duty and monitor students as they enter or exit the classroom.
6. Start and end every class session with a pleasant greeting such as *"Good morning 8-4's" or "Have a good day."*
7. Speak in a normal voice at all times when interacting with students. Never yell. Remember, students are responsible for hearing you.
8. Stand or sit with good posture, particularly when students display inappropriate behavior.
9. Give students directions on how to move around in the classroom. Do not allow students to walk in a manner that result in physical contact with other students.
10. Do not allow students to stand in front of your desk blocking your view of the rest of the group.
11. Do not repeat rules over and over. Say what you mean and mean what you say. When possible, respond to a student or students displaying inappropriate behavior by *saying nothing* and simply staring at the student or students as you document behavior.
12. Do not tolerate students talking when you are talking. If this occurs, respond with a question such as *"Why are you talking without permission?"* Document the

behavior.

13. Do not attempt to continue a lesson when students are disruptive. Stop the lesson and document behavior.

14. Redefine terms that represent disruptive behavior. (example: *fighting is 'touching another student without a teacher's permission' or 'touching another student in a negative manner'*)

15. Be aware at all times how your actions affect *respectful students* as you interact with students displaying inappropriate behavior.

16. Contact parents and administrators as infrequently as possible to resolve problems with students who display inappropriate behavior. Empower yourself by maintaining a classroom environment that's conducive to educating students.

17. If applicable, do not interrupt a class session in progress to contact a parent by telephone when a student displays inappropriate behavior. Consider the rights of respectful students who should not be exposed to hearing this type of conversation that in many instances is unproductive and results in a student acting even worse.

18. If possible, work with co-workers to develop strategies for monitoring students who are disruptive in more than one classroom. (discussed in Chapter 6)

19. Develop new behavior codes as needed. Use lines on the letter/codes sheet containing codes or use the letter/codes sheet containing no codes to create a set of behavior codes.

Remember, you must be the teacher in charge of the classroom until you resign or retire. Do what's necessary to insure this is the best experience it can be for you and all students you encounter.

7

Cooperative Monitoring: Grade Level & School Wide

Cooperative monitoring is effective for monitoring the behavior of individual students who display unruly behavior in more than one classroom or different areas of a school such as a lunchroom, etc. It can be implemented by using a **documentation sheet**. A personalized documentation sheet will give administrators, teachers and other staff persons opportunities to describe in detail the behavior of one student. It provides a *quick-read* by summarizing information that may actually be detailed on several referral forms and/or separate sheets of paper. A documentation sheet is most effective if two or more people work as a team to implement its use.

A team of administrators, teachers and other staff persons who work together can reduce the stress and isolation that's felt by many teachers who struggle to handle unruly students. It's been proven students respond better to behavioral expectations if they know school staff persons are working together to monitor their behavior. A team effort can also improve conferences with parents, particularly parents who say, *"You're the only person my child's having a problem with."* However, it's important to understand that, although it's great to have several people working together as a team, a team effort can start with just two people who are willing to work together.

The first person I teamed with was a wonderful teacher named Brenda Edwards. We taught the same eighth grade classes prior to her death in 1995. I had already established folders for each class that I taught by the time Brenda asked to work with me to monitor our students. Each folder contained documentation sheets that I set up for students who were causing behavior problems in more than one class or other areas of the school. I took it upon myself to inform other teachers, lunch aides, etc. that they were welcome to come into my room, access folders and record information on documentation sheets as needed. It wasn't difficult for me to take on the role of *captain of documentation sheets folders for eight grade students* because by this time I had already been placed in charge of several end of the school year eight grade activities. Eighth grade students were also responsive to my *demands* that they behave in other classes if teachers requested my help with problem students. Most students didn't care very much for being sent to my room if they were causing behavior problems in other teacher's rooms. Working with Brenda was a wonderful experience. Our classrooms were located on opposite ends of the same hallway. We faithfully performed hall duty according to the hall passing procedure I developed and controlled student movement in the entire hall area where our classrooms were located. Students literally *stopped on a dime* before entering the hall area where we were located. When we performed hall duty we had discipline charts in our hands for both of our classes that were exiting and both classes that were entering our classrooms. We also utilized blank charts to document students who were not in our classes if they came down our hall area displaying disruptive behavior. Although Brenda was the first teacher I teamed with to manage groups of students there were other teachers in the building who also implemented the plan in their prospective locations. I had a wonderful experience teaching in the Detroit Public Schools middle school that I worked for during those years.

It was a wonderful experience working with Brenda to manage the behavior of several groups of students. Although I rarely ever had parent conferences concerning student behavior, Brenda enjoyed being able to access a student's documentation sheet to reinforce information during conferences she had with parents. She was literally able to speak on behalf of whoever logged information on a student's sheet she accessed. This proved to be a powerful intervention strategy that spared administrators on more than one occasion from having to become involved in mediating a parent-teacher conference. My role in all of this would prove invaluable during the 1991-92 school year when I was asked to take a temporary assignment as a math and science unit head for grade eight. The request resulted from my immediate supervisor being promoted to an assistant principal at another school right after the beginning of that school year. She recommended me for the position and, after about a week of thinking it over, I accepted. This gave me the opportunity to use documentation sheets to centralize student behavior information for all eighth grade students in the school. It was so successful that I started working with the unit head for grades six and seven to centralize behavior information for those grades. We had a wonderful school year that resulted in a quieter building, improved tests scores, teachers who were more motivated to work, etc.

Since retiring in 2001 I've had the opportunity to work with schools to centralize student behavior information for more effective management of student behavior problems. Cooperative monitoring continues to be the key for smooth implementation of a centralized plan. If staff people work together, it works. If there's a breakdown in staff people working together, it doesn't. However, no matter how many schools implement plans for entire staffs to work together, it's important to remember the following statement: *Where there is two, there can be a team.*

•Implementing Cooperative Monitoring•

To implement cooperative monitoring duplicate copies of the documentation sheet located in the supplement. If students are assigned to homerooms and their schedule of classes is based on classes traveling in groups from class to class, a homeroom teacher can prepare a documentation sheets folder for a group of students. It is recommended that the folder contain the following items.

1. an alphabetized class list
2. a minimum of 10 copies of a documentation sheet

A decision can be made about where folders will be kept. The location should provide easy access for teachers and other staff persons and no access for students. When I taught school there were years when each homeroom teacher kept the folder for his/her group. However, there were years when I kept all 8th grade folders in my classroom. Teachers and other staff persons were able to access folders as needed.

Once folders are set up, any staff person can implement a documentation sheet for an unruly student. When I taught middle school this was usually initiated by a teacher who accessed the appropriate folder for an unruly student and checked the class list located in the folder to see if a sheet had already been started on the student. If started, the teacher documented information concerning the student's behavior. (see example 7-1; pg.111) If not, the teacher wrote a check mark (√) or date next to the student's name on the alphabetized list. This readily identified a student as having a documentation sheet already set up for continuous logging of student behavior information. If there was no check mark or date by a student's name on an alphabetized list, the teacher placed a check mark or date by the student's name, started a documentation sheet for the student by writing the student's name on a documentation sheet and documented information in appropriate columns on the student's documentation sheet. Documentation sheets in each folder were alphabetized at all times for quick and easy access.

Once the plan has been implemented teachers, etc. should periodically meet together to discuss how documented information can be used. The following list represents strategies that were used by teachers I worked with to improve student behavior.

1. A teacher schedules a conference with a student on behalf of several teachers who documented information on the student's documentation sheet. The teacher documents whether or not the student commits to improving his/her behavior.

2. A teacher who refers a student to an administrator can provide an administrator with a duplicate copy of the student's documentation sheet. This can reinforce an administrator's opportunity to make an administrative decision that's based on a student's behavior pattern that's been established by all who wrote on a student's documentation sheet.

3. Teachers can make documentation sheets available for school social workers, psychologists and other staff persons who may find the information useful.

4. A teacher can access a student's documentation sheet for a parent-teacher conference. This can reinforce student behavior information that's discussed with a parent.

5. A group of teachers can schedule a conference with a parent, student and/or administrator and discuss information contained on a student's documentation sheet. A decision or decisions can then be made to bring a resolution to behavior problems that are occurring with the student.

6. A group of teachers and an administrator can meet with one or several documented students to discuss information contained on documentation sheets. Decisions can be made about steps that must be taken to correct the behavior of these students. I strongly recommend this strategy or a similar strategy that eliminates the need to involve entire student populations in mass assemblies to resolve behavior problems that are the result of a select group of students.

•Improving Student Behavior In Hall Areas•

Although I briefly discussed student behavior in hall areas in a previous chapter, I'd like to discuss this in more detail here. A team of teachers and/or administrators can improve students' behavior in halls by working together to implement a discipline plan specifically designed for the hall area. Although this plan is a component of cooperative monitoring that's being presented in this chapter, it's important that it is treated as a separate component so that it receives the respect it deserves. The result should be implementation of a hall discipline plan such that students cannot brush off implementation of it as if it's no big deal as they travel through hall areas. I continue to see too much of a *'I think I'm out at a park behavior'* from students who behave in halls areas as if *they have no place to go and no time to be there.*

Poor student behavior in hall areas will not change until students understand that school staff persons are working together to monitor student behavior in hall areas and *they're not joking* about expecting students to act right. The plan should be implemented in such a way that staff persons are not expected to be responsible for *moving students along*. Students should be totally responsible for the *moving along part of this process* and staff persons should be totally responsible for written monitoring of student's behavior if they violate rules established for movement in hall areas. Students should be informed that the role of staff persons in hall areas is to *pleasantly greet* students by nodding, speaking, etc. as students *quietly walk* through hall areas during allotted time periods from class to class, etc. I'd like to take time here to make a very strong statement because I continue to see too many situations where student behavior in hall areas is not seriously factored into school-wide plans for managing student behavior.

People, we need to wake up and get serious about consistently working together to manage student behavior in hall areas!

To this day I still believe it sets the tone for what happens in a school such that it's a major factor for whether or not a school's overall environment is conducive to educating students.

This paragraph describes the plan that I *consistently* implemented for the hall area during the years I taught middle school. Today I continue to thoroughly discuss the plan when I conduct classroom management workshops. It's that important to me. The plan can be implemented as follows. When performing hall duty each teacher should use a folder containing four or five blank chart copies and several passes that will be used to write unexcused or excused passes for students detained in the hall area. (Chart copies are made by duplicating the 8 ½ in. by 11in. grid located in the supplement.) The folder should also contain a letter/codes sheet or set of codes selected for hall monitoring. (review pages 60 and 95) The plan can be strategically implemented by each staff person who's involved in monitoring by doing the following; *detain at least two or three unruly students a day until word spreads that administrators and teachers are serious about students behaving in the hall area.* There is a strategic basis for stopping a specified number of students. Students who are stopped will tell other students what happened. Therefore, consistent implementation insures the plan will work as students *help spread the word.* The hall area discipline plan should be explained to all students during an assembly and reinforced by individual teachers. The plan can be reinforced even more if administrators visit individual classrooms. It is recommended that the following rules be clarified and discussed.

1. Students must wear identification cards containing students' photos or they can be stopped by staff persons and cited for insubordination. (Identification cards should be provided by the school.)

2. Students who display inappropriate behavior can be detained by a teacher who will document students behavior. They should then be sent to their next class with unexcused tardy passes to show they were detained for inappropriate behavior in the hall area. They should be marked tardy because they are at fault for not making it to class on time. However, under special circumstances, teachers have the option to write excused tardy passes.

3. Students will receive an in-house detention, be suspended from school for one day, etc. if stopped twice by any staff person or caught running from a staff person who attempts to detain them for unruly behavior in the hall area. If an administrator receives several referrals for a student, the student will be excluded from participation in school activities, suspended for one or more days from school, etc.

When a teacher or other staff person detains a student for displaying unruly behavior in the hall area, a discipline chart for hall behavior should be scanned to see if the student's name has already been written on the chart. If not, the student's name and behavioral information should be documented using selected behavior codes. (names will be un-alphabetized) The teacher should follow the procedure established for unruly behavior in the hall area. If a referral is written the teacher should take or send it to the appropriate administrator as soon as possible.

A common problem displayed by students in the hall area is *running.* In many schools an *invisible track* is not located in the gym. It's located where, *in the hall area.* I'm not trying to make light of the problem but I can't begin to tell you how many times I've felt a *breeze* behind my back when students ran past me as I performed hall duty. It felt pretty good on days when it was much too hot to be in a building that lacked air-conditioning. Okay, back to being serious. I will admit students running in halls can be unnerving, particularly if you are trying to detain a student for inappropriate behavior and the student is not enrolled in one of the classes you teach. However, I always remember the old saying, *"Where there's a will, there's a way."* It didn't make any sense to get angry because I couldn't detain or identify a *running* student. I reminded myself I was only one human being and decided to *lock in* on identifying one student if a student or several students ran. This worked most of the time. I'd document information on the hall discipline chart and write a question mark in the area for the student's name. Sooner or later (usually sooner) the student would come my way again and I was able to get the student's name and resolve the problem. Something else happened that made the situation easier. Other students who respected my efforts to manage students behaviorally would sometimes identify a student who ran.

Students who ran always seemed surprised when I stopped them a second time and described behavior I could now put a name with. They were also surprised at how calm I was and couldn't understand why I didn't look angry. If there was a hall discipline plan I followed it. If not, I usually gave the student warning, documented information and sent him/her to class with an excused pass. I didn't write unexcused passes if there was no plan for monitoring students' behavior in the hall area. However, even if other teachers didn't monitor students in the hall area I knew detained students would help me because they would *spread the word* that I meant business. I had no intention of spending twenty-five or thirty years listening to excessive noise near my classroom.

Some teachers and other staff persons will say a hall plan that requires they stop students is too much work for an already *overloaded* workload. However, I'm saying health issues are involved in not monitoring students in the hall area. A headache at the end of a school day is a common complaint of teachers who listen to noise in halls day in and day out. I'm saying a hall plan can be implemented and, if necessary, will work for a teacher who decides to *go it on his/her own* without the help of other staff persons. I'm not saying it's easy but I am saying it will minimize the noise level near your classroom if you are a teacher who has to *go it alone.* I handled Discipline folders for my classes and a folder for monitoring other students in the hall area. I made a commitment to maintain order in *my area* of the hall and utilized the plan the entire time I taught school. I will admit there were years when I was the only teacher consistently utilizing this strategy. It worked the majority of the time and minimized the amount of unruly behavior I was exposed to. Most students didn't want to be bothered with being stopped by me so they were quieter when they were in my presence. This was the case even when I taught high school students.

I never accepted the belief nothing could be done about students' behavior in halls if administrative input was not a factor. I informed students in halls they were obligated to respect all staff persons in the building. I utilized my prep hour to report information to an administrator. This resulted in less behavior problems as students spread the word to their peers that they should *avoid me* in the hall area. I literally observed students turn a corner and, when they saw me, turn and walk in the opposite direction. I'm going to *keep it real* by telling you I had no problem with their *change of heart* decision. There were several years where it was *nice and quiet* near my classroom the majority of a school year. I loved it!

•Administrative Use of Discipline Charts & Documentation Sheets•

Discipline Charts and Documentation Sheets can be used to centralize *behavior* information for all students in a school. As I previously stated, I did not teach math for the 1991-92 school year. I accepted a temporary administrative position as a math and science unit head for grade eight students with the condition that I could return to the classroom if I wasn't satisfied with the position. To my surprise it turned out to be a wonderful year. I was given the opportunity with the full support of my principal to implement all components of the classroom monitoring system I had developed and could continue to add new components to the plan. Although I never planned to become a classroom management consultant, that year was probably the year that locked in the foundation for the work I do today.

I will clarify here that I accepted the role of substitute administrator with a strong stipulation that the main component of my work would be to establish a centralized student behavior plan for grade eight students. Although I was put in charge of math and science, I believed that teachers for those subjects were the true experts in their areas and what they really needed was someone who would make sure students would act right so they'd have the opportunity to teach in their individual classrooms. Our school had not become involved in implementation of any team-teaching strategies and, although there were discussions during staff meetings, workshops conducted by visiting consultants, etc. concerning implementation of team-teaching, there was great reluctance to do so due to problems with student behavior. My principal was quite interested in the concept of team-teaching but he pretty well knew it wouldn't happen unless teachers felt there wouldn't be problems with student behavior. Therefore, I would soon move in a direction of implementing the plan I developed in such a way that it resolved student behavior problems for the entire school.

One of the first things I did was go to each 8th grade class and explain behavioral expectations and the procedure that would be used for documenting referrals received from teachers and other staff persons. I also explained that consequences for unruly behavior would be based on a student's behavior in all classes and areas of the school. I wanted students to know in advance what to expect so they could make an *informed decision* about how to behave. I explained to students that if they were sent to me they'd have a choice of two responses for a written referral, *'yes' you did it or 'no' you didn't.* It was fairly obvious what the response would be if they came to my office. I clarified I wouldn't tolerate *lengthy speeches* for behavior problems that occurred in classrooms or other areas of the school.

I established a documentation sheet for every student referred by a teacher or other staff person in the building. Some students had existing documentation sheets as a result of the plan being implemented while I was still teaching in the classroom. If I determined that it was necessary to prepare an updated documentation sheet for sheets already established, I set up new documentation sheets and transferred information in order of dates to merge information that was written before and I became a substitute administrator with information that was written afterwards. I believed it was critical for students to relate to their behavior as part of an ongoing pattern that they could make the decision to correct for the sake of all teachers, students, etc. therefore, I talked with custodians, lunchroom workers, etc. and asked them to report students who displayed inappropriate behavior. I was concerned that students consistently display appropriate behavior throughout the building. I didn't want students wasting time trying to decide when or where they could misbehave. Everything I did was explained to students. When a student was sent to me I accessed the student's documentation sheet from my file and reviewed previously written information. I always started a discussion by asking a student to answer *'yes'* or *'no'* to acknowledge if he/she *committed the crime.* Then I discussed the student's *current* behavior problem. After the discussion I logged information on the documentation sheet and explained consequences for the behavior. Then, I informed the student of consequences for the next behavior problem if one should occur. As stated before, the goal was to establish consistency for appropriate consequences that addressed a student's *overall behavior pattern.* When students left my office I also wanted them to think about what they needed to do to avoid future problems. Most conferences were held without a teacher present because teachers understood I was more interested in addressing a student's behavior pattern than just focusing on a student's behavior in one classroom. I also didn't want classes interrupted. Therefore, teachers had the option to attend or not attend conferences. However, I encouraged them not to forego class sessions to do it.

During a conference with a student, if I saw that the student had three or more dates of information documented I gave the student a letter to take home requesting a conference with a parent. Again, it was not mandatory for teachers to attend this conference. Teachers were able to access information documented at their leisure and were always aware of what took place with their students. When a parent came in I discussed a student's overall behavior pattern. I made it clear that the student was having problems with more than one teacher or staff person. This conference took a lot of pressure off individual teachers and resulted in parents displaying better behavior when they realized information was centralized. They understood they couldn't *get away with verbally attacking one teacher.* It was rare that I saw a parent display inappropriate behavior but when I did I dated and documented it on back of a student's documentation sheet as a *'parental response.'* During this conference parents were informed that the student would be suspended from school as necessary to insure other students had an opportunity to learn without being continuously distracted as a result of the student's behavior.

After approximately a month of working in the position things were going so well that I had time to relax on my lunch hour and read a newspaper without a teacher and/or student suddenly rushing into my office to resolve a problem. Students absolutely did not want to be sent to my office. They hated *that sheet* that contained detailed information about their behavior. If a student's behavior was *really bad*, it was necessary to use two or more documentation sheets to log information. The sheets were stapled together as needed.

During this time I also had the opportunity to talk with individual teachers and, when necessary, request they stay calm and maintain professionalism when interacting with unruly students. I asked them to not be repetitive and to expect students to follow rules. If applicable, I requested they be willing to work on improving their actions when interacting with students. For instance, I requested they *stop yelling* if this was a behavior they employed to handle unruly students. I assured them they could send students to me for all behavior problems as long as they made the effort to maintain professionalism when interacting with students.

Did strategies I implemented work? Absolutely! Did they require a great deal of work on my part? Initially, yes! But once students understood there was *no deviation in behavioral expectations*, that *consistency was the order of the day*, they settled down and started working in classrooms. It worked so well that I was able to hold students accountable for respecting substitute teachers and not leaving classrooms unless they had appropriate passes signed by teachers. I also started working with the sixth and seventh grade math and science unit head to resolve behavior problems throughout the building such as violation of the dress code policy for students, unruly behavior in the lunchroom, etc. Individual folders containing discipline charts were established and used to monitor specific behaviors. These folders were established by requesting each homeroom teacher write a master chart that listed names of all students in his/her homerooms. Each homeroom teacher was given three chart copies to write an alphabetized class list. Completed chart sets were then duplicated and used as needed to established folders for monitoring specific behaviors. Each folder contained a set of charts for the entire school. For example, a folder was set up to monitor students who violated the school's dress code. Any staff person could detain a student who was dressed inappropriately and send the student to an administrator who would log information on the appropriate chart in the dress code folder. Two violations resulted in a one-day suspension from school. *Centralization, centralization! The left hand must know what the right hand's doing!* That's the key for everything running smoothly.

One of the major components of the newly created centralized monitoring system resulted from teaching staff working together and agreeing on twelve rules that incorporated all rules established in individual classrooms. Teachers could still post rules in classrooms but the goal was to get students on the same page for following rules throughout the school. All students were given a copy of the twelve rules that contained a cutoff section for parents to sign acknowledging receipt. The cutoffs were returned to me and information logged on a student's homeroom chart located in a folder established for monitoring Random Activities for all students. (Monitoring random activities will be explained in Chapter 8.)

It was a wonderful school year because I was able to take the monitoring system I used in the classroom and expand its use to the entire school. There was an overall improvement in student behavior that school year. There was also improvement in standardized test scores. The principal asked me to consider Acting for the next school year. It was his plan to have me become an official Unit Head if I so desired. However, I'm a firm believer things happen for a reason. I loved the work I did that particular school year but I missed teaching. As it turned out the principal became principal of another school before the start of the next school year and I returned to the classroom.

A team of teachers and administrators working together is a powerful force for resolving the discipline crisis occurring in schools. Administrators have a tremendous job to do that include empathizing with overworked and underpaid teachers. When teachers believe they are truly respected by administrators there's just about nothing they won't do to improve a school's environment. Administrators must give teachers opportunities to express their concerns. Teachers must be involved in selecting and approving plans to resolve discipline problems. There must be respect shown for daily attempts to implement lessons without teachers being *pulled* from classrooms in the middle of lessons to attend conferences on behalf of unruly students. This is not fair to respectful students who lose out on being educated.

Let's think about it for one minute. If you were head of a hospital, would you suddenly *pull* a brain surgeon out of surgery in the middle of an operation on a patient's brain? No you wouldn't! You understand the importance of the surgery being completed without interruption. Are students in classrooms less important? No they aren't! Teachers struggle year after year after year to *operate* on students' brains by implanting knowledge. (Isn't that how brain surgeons became surgeons?) Sometimes the *operation* is repeated over and over on *hardheaded students* who don't get it the first or second time around because they are behaviorally out of control. Administrators must give teachers the same respect they would give a brain surgeon. Pulling a teacher out of a classroom in the middle of a lesson is no less detrimental than pulling a surgeon out of an operating room in the middle of a surgery. It may take longer to see the damage to students left in classrooms when teachers are suddenly pulled out but it will show up sooner or later. This one act in itself has cost students throughout the nation years and years of precious class time that's lost forever. I wrote the previous statement in my second classroom management book. Now here we are eight years later and not very much has changed.

To resolve the discipline crisis teachers and administrators must *get on the same page at the same time.* Unruly student behavior is a major crisis occurring in classrooms throughout the nation. Effective monitoring of unruly student behavior is crucial to eradicate this dilemma. Personalized documentation sheets can be used to solve the problem and it's now possible to create computerized documentation sheets that all staff persons could access as needed to input or review student behavior information. Most teachers have access to computers and could input information without leaving classrooms.

Example 7-1 below shows a documentation sheet that was prepared for student Yolanda Lewis. Information contained on Yolanda's sheet includes information that was written on a discipline chart that resulted in a referral being written and sent to an administrator. This example clearly shows that Yolanda was given ample opportunities to correct her behavior before being faced with a possibility of being suspended from school.

EXAMPLE 7-1 (front)

DOCUMENTATION SHEET

STUDENT'S NAME/GRADE: Yolanda Lewis /8-4

STAFF PERSON	DATE:HOUR	BEHAVIOR	ACTION TAKEN	see other side(√)
Mr. Bivens	9/25 : 1st	excessive tardies	-letter sent home -referred to counselor	
Ms. Taylor (lunch aide)	9/28 : 4th	continues to sit at wrong table during lunch hour	verbal warning	
Ms. Danniels	10/4 : 6th	verbal outbursts and non-participation in class	-talked with student -gave verbal warning	
Mrs. Dotson	10/11 : 2nd	all of the above	mass conference held with students on 10/11	√
Mr. Jackson	10/19 : 4th	excessive rule violations in classroom	parent-teacher-student conference scheduled	√
Mrs. Dotson	10/29 : 2nd	continues verbal outbursts in classroom	written referral sent to Mr. Hamilton (admin.)	√
Mr. Hamilton	10/30	all of the above	conference requested with parent on 10/31	√

EXAMPLE 7-1 (back)

(Documentation Sheet:other side)

10/11 (Mrs. Dotson)-discussed behavior pattern logged on Documentation Sheet and possible action to be taken if poor behavior continues -Docu. Sheet mailed home

10/20 (Mr. Jackson)-conference scheduled with parent and student on 10/23 to discuss disruptive behavior pattern (see attached referral copy) -sent written referral to Mr. Hamilton (no action required if conference request is completed and poor behavior ceases)

10/30 (Mr. Hamilton)-student will be given a 3 day exclusion from school if conference request is incomplete or behavior continues

8

Monitoring Academic & Random Activities

The 8½ in. x 11in. grid located in the supplement can be duplicated to prepare charts to monitor several activities that include the discipline chart that was described in chapter 4. Using a chart to monitor student behavior can definitely lay a foundation for being able to use charts to monitor other activities such as activities for small group instruction, individualized assignments for advanced students, game activities, etc. In this chapter I will describe two activities I monitored by using charts. The first activity was implemented for advance students who, although they were very good math students, they weren't necessary at grade level mathematically. The second activity was implemented to provide all students with opportunities to practice computational skills based on individual needs. Charts gave me the opportunity to track both activities in such a way that every student was able to progress at his/her own pace. I knew at all times what each student was working on, whether progress was being made, etc. It was a beautiful experience for me and extremely motivational for students. It resolved a lot of behavior issues that occurred among advance students and students whose math skills were not as advanced.

•Activity#1: Individualized Math Assignment For Advanced Students•

Incorporating individualized assignments into classroom instruction can enhance a teacher's efforts to keep students focused on learning. Most educators will agree that individualized assignments are excellent for students who need skill strengthening and students who display exceptional academic talent. However, many teachers are concerned about how to accomplish this task without creating a burdensome amount of work.

Chart copies containing names of all students can be used to set up the activity. (Review Chapter 4 as needed on how to prepare chart copies.) Example 8-1; pg.114 shows a chart that I set up to monitor the progress of advance students who worked through a chapter in a math textbook. The chapter, Percentages, was not presented to the entire class. Selected students were required to complete all assigned class work unless otherwise instructed. They were also informed they had to maintain a grade of C+ or better and display acceptable behavior to participate in this activity. Students worked at their own pace with minimal guidance from me. They also worked cooperatively with each other. The individualized assignment gave advanced students an opportunity to *catch up* on math concepts they should have already learned and also motivated other students to work harder.

The individualized assignment was easy to prepare and monitor. Pages of a chapter and worksheets were listed in columns on the chart. When a student completed a lesson, the student used the teacher's manual or a set of prepared answer sheets to check his/her work. Students asked questions as needed to work through the chapter. I asked follow up questions as I deemed necessary to insure students understood assignments. Completed lessons were signed by me and documented on the chart. I requested a parental signature on completed work. Students were instructed to keep this work in a folder separate from regularly assigned class work. When an assigned chapter was completed a student was given a follow up quiz or test. A new chapter was selected as needed and another chart set up for continuous implementation of individualized assignments.

Students were given extra credit for successfully completing assignments. However, several of these students were earning A's in math. Therefore, they were informed that the work would give them an opportunity to catch up or advance in math skills. Several of my former students who worked on individualized assignments returned to informed me they were placed in advance or accelerated math classes after entering high school.

The individualized assignment activity also served to keep me on top of my math skills. I was able to *brush up* on concepts I rarely had the opportunity to teach due to students who were usually two to three years behind in math skills. Several of these students enjoyed taking a *sneak preview* of chapters assigned for advanced students. It motivated them to work harder. All students understood that I wanted them to do their best. That's all I ever required of students.

The individualized assignment activity was excellent throughout a school year as students were given continuous opportunities to channel their energies in a positive direction. It also proved to be a wonderful challenge for me as I worked to *keep pace* with advanced students while doing my best to meet the needs of students who weren't as advanced.

EXAMPLE 8-1

INDIVIDUALIZED ASSIGNMENT CHART (CHAPTER 8/PERCENTAGES)

√	Section 8-4 / Page 1 of 3	pgs.1-2	wksht 1	pgs.3-4	wksht 2	pgs.5-6	wksht 3	pgs 7-8	wksht 4	pgs.9-10	chapt. review	test 1	test 2
√	Abrams, Todd	X	X	X	X								
	Farley, Dan												
	Jones, Brenda												
	Lewis, Yolanda												
√	Stewart, Janet	X	X	X	X	X	X	X	X	X			
√	Washington, Brian	X	X	X	X	X	X	X	X	X	X	X	
	Young, Sheila												

•Activity 2: A Math Game Activity For All Students•

The math game activity was implemented to provide students with a fun way to practice computational skills based on each student's skill level. I knew students enjoyed playing board games. There were also students who enjoyed drawing during class time when they were should have been working on math assignments. So I decided to *tap* into what they enjoyed and use it to their advantage. Several students, including advanced students were tired of always working problems in a math textbook. The activity proved to be a win-win and resulted in advanced students mastering computational skills that were more advanced than what I taught during the school year. I started the game with students in grade 8. Some students who were low in math skills started by practicing addition of whole numbers while more advanced students started by practicing addition of positive and negative fractions.

The math game activity was implemented by having students work in pairs to create and draw a 'board game' on legal size manila folders. When this part of the activity was completed, each student was required to have his/her own copy of a game. Students were instructed not to restrict use of the board by writing math problems on the board. They were instructed to develop the board by designing areas that players would move around, through, across, etc. Then they were instructed to create instructions for moving back and forth, scoring, etc. as players move around a board. If a board was completed according to my instructions, the board could be used in any classroom for any subject. I had the responsibility of preparing problems and answers for the activity. This was done by writing math problems and answers on index cards. Students played in groups of two to four students. Each group was given a set of index cards that had problems written on half the set and answers written on the other half. Problem cards were labeled P1, P2, P3, etc. Matching answer cards were labeled A1, A2, A3, etc. Problems and answers were written on the other side of each labeled card. They were placed into games with labeled sides up. Students were occasionally allowed to shuffle problem cards but had to keep answer cards in order for quick access to answers as students solved problems. The average number of problems prepared for a game was 30.

I established one rule that pertained to the academic portion of game sessions. When students started playing they were instructed to set up a game log that would be used to solve problems. They had to show work for all problems solved so I could check work as I moved around the room to insure students were solving all problems pulled in a game session. If seven problems were pulled in a game session with a group of students, every student in the group had to show written work for how all seven problems were solved. This made it easy for me to move through all groups during a session and check the majority of students' work. When necessary I could take a student out of a game, quickly work with the student and then have the student return to the group to continue playing the game. Monitoring written work was not difficult because students were required to write neat, date a log in the margin area to show where a game session began and draw a line to show where a session ended. Students were also required to write C's and X's so I'd know right away if a student needed help when I looked at written work. If a problem was marked wrong students were instructed to write the correct answer by the X, not erase the problem and work a new problem for the problem that was marked wrong. I wanted students to be able to compare both problems so they could identify errors. Students enjoyed the activity to the extent that I had no problem with students raising their hands during game sessions when they needed help.

The game activity was definitely a motivational activity that students who displayed poor behavior were excluded from. The homework assignment for the game was simply to study problems that students had trouble with. Sometimes I gave or students requested follow up problems for homework. If a student felt ill, had a problem with excessive absence, behavior, etc. the student was exclude from the game activity for one or more game sessions. I set up an area in the room and gave applicable students math worksheet assignments that required minimal input from me. The worksheets were not a punishment assignment so there were occasions when *fun worksheets* were assigned for completion.

You may ask why I've taken the time to explain this activity in detail. Because I realized years ago that a game board of this type could be used to improve students' academic skills in several subjects. This could result in a real boost in standardized test scores throughout a school and it doesn't hurt that it's a cost effective activity. This year I had the opportunity to present this activity to an eighth grade math teacher in a school I did math consultant work for. She immediately recognized the value of the activity.

She implemented it in her classroom and explained it to teachers who taught other subjects. The interest was so great that the plan is for the game activity to be implemented throughout the school during the next school year.

Example 8-2 below shows an example of how to set up and monitor the game activity. The example covers a three week period. An explanation is typed below the chart that describes how the activity is implemented.

EXAMPLE 8-2

Math Game Chart

	Section 8-2 Page 1 of 3	*Game Partners*	*Game Session 9/13*	*Game Session 9/20*	*Game Session 9/27*						
1	*Abrams, Rob*	6	6	absent	----						
2	*Farlan, Dana*	4-7	4	4-7-6	1-7						
3	*Jones, Reva*	5	5	5	4-5						
4	*Lewis, Alana*	----	----	----	----						
5	*Stanley, Joe*	----	----	----	----						
6	*Waverly, Joi*	----	----	----	ill						
7	*Young, Dave*	----	absent	----	----						

Note: A pencil is used to write on the chart because students change groups based on mastery of math skills.

Column 1: Students are numbered in the first column on the left.

Column 2: List of student names.

Column 3: Students are assigned temporary game partners based on pre-tests, etc. to determine math skills they need to practice.

- Start with Rob Abrams. Move alphabetically through student names and select all students who will be assigned to play in the same group as Rob Abrams. Write their student numbers in column 3 (game partners) next to Rob's name. Joi Waverly has been assigned to play with Rob. Therefore, her student number is written in column 3 next to Rob's name to show they will play in the same group. A line is drawn next to her name in column 3 to show she's been assigned to play in a group. Return to the beginning of the list of student names after selecting all students who will play with Rob Abrams. Starting with Rob Abrams again, alphabetically move down the list of names until you come to the first available student who has not been assigned to play in a group. In this example it will be Dana Farlan. (Remember: There were no numbers written next to Dana's name when you started with Rob Abrams and identified his game partner.) Follow the same procedure that was used to select game partners for Rob Abrams. Alana Lewis and Dave Young have been assigned to play in the same group as Dana. Their student numbers have been placed in column 3 next to her name and lines drawn next to their names in column 3 to show they've been assigned. Continue this process until all students are assigned to groups.

Column 4: On 9/13 students played the first math game session. Dave Young was absent that day.

Column 5: On 9/20 students played the second game session. Rob Abrams was absent that day. Therefore, Joi Waverly was temporarily re-assigned to play in the group with Dana, Alana and Dave. Joi's re-assignment works because her group is practicing the same problems that Dana, Alana and Dave are practicing. (I usually made at least three sets of the same cards to insure I had enough sets so group did not have more than four students playing.) The chart shows that Dave Young was present that day. Although he was absent on 9/13 his group assignment has not changed. His game log will show that he did not have an opportunity to do math problems that were pulled when students played on 9/13. Therefore it may take him longer to master problems in the set of cards his group is playing with. This can result in some students advancing to play with other groups before he advances. If this happens he may be reassigned to play with another group that's using the same set of cards he's playing with. (I will discuss how I resolved students not having to solve problems more than once in a game set.)

Column 6: On 9/27 students played the third math game session. The chart shows that Rob Abrams was present that day but he's temporarily re-assigned to play with Dana and Dave. Alana advances to play in the group with Reva and Joe. Joi is ill so she sits in an area reserved for students who don't play. She quietly works on a fun worksheet and from time to time lays her head on a desk as needed.

(Note: The total number of students in each column on game days must add up to 7 no matter how the numbers are switched around due to reassigning game partners.)

The math game activity was a win-win and continuously challenged me to make whatever revisions needed to keep it going. Students contributed by suggesting strategies that helped smooth out the rough edges as the activity progressed. For example, I had to resolve the *solving problems issue* so students wouldn't have to repeat solving problems they had done in previous game sessions. The game log took care of this because students had to circle problem numbers as they solved problems. This made it easier and quicker for students to scan game logs and identify which problems had already been completed when problems were pulled during a game session. Students and I decided that if a student's game log showed a problem had been correctly solved in a previous game session, the student would automatically be given credit for the problem based on the rules for the current board game being played on. This kept students motivated if they had to sit for a few minutes and wait on other students to complete a problem. Although time limits for completing problems varied, there were definite time limits set for how long a student would have to complete a problem. Students were very creative with what they used to monitor time. I remember one group actually used an hour glass to set a time limit. I loved it!

Taking the time to describe the details for how I implemented the math game activity was a major decision for me. But it's such an important activity because the game board can be used for other subject areas. It's a simple matter of preparing sets of problem and answer cards that contain whatever concepts, etc. the preparer wants to provide practice for. For example, if a reading teacher has a list of 500 words students should learn in a school year, just imagine how much fun students would have if words and definitions were put into a game of this type. Today there are wonderful materials available for creating game boards that are more durable than manila folders. However, manila folders are still more affordable than many materials that can be purchased and I believe many students today will still appreciate and take care of what they create. My students prepared game boards at the beginning of a school year and, after all the wear and tear, still had them at the end of a school year. Today, I still have copies of duplicate game boards that I requested some students make for me to keep. I give teachers opportunities to see these boards when I discuss the math game activity during workshops or visits to schools.

I will conclude discussion of the math game activity with the directions for how to create a game board, game log, etc. Again, it's important that the game board is multi-purpose and is prepared so it can be used for subjects other than math. (Reminder: This activity can be implemented by parents, persons in charge of after school programs, etc.)

Directions for person in charge (teacher, parent, etc.) and game participants (students, etc.)

1) A game participant should draw a rough draft of a game on paper. (use pencils) Do not draw negative images or write inappropriate words on the rough draft.

2) A game participant should develop rules for moving around the board, accumulating points, etc. (Reminder: Do not write problems on the rough draft of the board. Problems should be provided for a game by a person in charge.)

3) A rough draft of a game should receive final approval before being drawn on a manila folder, game board, etc. (approved by a person in charge of the activity)

4) A person in charge should prepare sets of problem and answer cards or designate others to do the same. (20-40 problems with answers are recommended per set.)

5) A person in charge should set up a game chart to monitor game participants during game sessions. (Use pencils to write on the chart.)

6) A person in charge should decide who will provide game pieces, spinners, etc.

7) A game participant should set up a game log to solve problems that will be provided for game sessions. (Staple approximately 10 sheets of line paper together.)

   a) The log should be dated at the beginning of each game session. A line should be drawn to show where a session ends.

   b) A game participant should solve all problems pulled during a game session. Each problem should be worked out on a game log. A person in charge should use a game chart to monitor a game session to insure all problems pulled during a game session are solved. A person in charge should also help a game participant who requests assistance during the activity. Brief tutoring should be provided in a location away from where the game is being played. A game participant should return to continue the game after brief tutoring. A person in charge should assign game participants to different groups as they master math skills.

   c) A person in charge should continue making problem and answer sets as needed. When necessary, make 3 or 4 sets of the same problem and answer cards.

   d) If applicable, a person in charge will establish an area in a room for game participants who cannot participate in a game session. (due to illness, excessive absence, behavior, etc.) Directions should be given to insure game participants behave appropriately. For example, game participants should be informed they cannot talk too loud or laugh disruptively during the activity. Behavior should be monitored on a discipline chart.

•Activity #3: Monitoring Random Activities•

A Random Activities Chart is excellent for monitoring classroom activities. A chart set containing an alphabetized class list can be used to set up this chart. (see Example

8-3; pg.120) In example 8-3 columns three and four are used to show students were given a class syllabus to take home at the beginning of a school year. An abbreviated heading for *class syllabus* is written in column three. Explanations for abbreviated headings and dates should be written on back of the chart. A check mark (√) is written in each student's box in column three to show that a student has been given a class syllabus. When the student returns the cutoff section of a syllabus that requires a parental signature, the date of return is written in the student's box in column four. Example 8-3 shows that all students except Janet Stewart were given a class syllabus on September 4th. Janet was absent so she received it on September 7th. The fourth column shows various dates for students as they returned the cutoff section of the class syllabus. It also shows that Todd and Janet did not return the syllabus cutoff. Other columns on the chart can be used to represent dates various handouts (news letters, report cards, etc.) are given to students to take home.

In example 8-3 columns five and six are used to write textbook assignments. These columns contain textbook numbers and the conditions of books assigned to students. The headings, *'assigned book#* and *book condition'* are written vertically at the top of the columns. Example 8-3 shows that book numbers 81-87 are assigned to students in section 8-4. It also shows the condition of each book assigned.

EXAMPLE 8-3

Random Activities Chart

	Section 8-4 Page 1 of 3	*Class Syl. 9/4*	*9/4 Syl. Cutoff ret.*	*Assigned Book #*	*Book condition*				
1	*Abrams, Todd*	√		81	Good				
2	*Farley, Dan*	√	9/12	82	Excellent				
3	*Jones, Brenda*	√	9/11	83	Fair				
4	*Lewis, Yolanda*	√	9/11	84	New				
5	*Stewart, Janet*	9/7		85	Excellent				
6	*Washington, Brian*	√	9/10	86	Good				
7	*Young, Sheila*	√	9/12	87	New				

There is no limit to how charts can be used. That's my belief. They enhanced my role as a classroom educator who provided students with opportunities to learn in an environment where unruly behavior was not tolerated. Using copies of the same chart for various activities simplified my work because I didn't have to write students' names over and over as I set up charts to monitor different activities.

•Activity 4: Writing A Class Activity Log •

A class activity log should be written by students to provide parents with accurate information about daily assignments, homework, dates quizzes and tests are given and sent home, scheduled assemblies, half days, etc. Writing a log represents one more opportunity for students to assume responsibility for keeping track of all assigned work and providing parents, etc. with information for assigned work and all activities that affect class sessions. A teacher should maintain a *master log* that contains *student log* information and any additional *teacher* information that a teacher needs to keep track of what happens with a group of students. When I taught school I was totally dependent on master logs. I taught five math classes daily and kept a separate log for each class. Master logs were kept in the same folders containing discipline charts. I logged assignments daily for each class to keep track of where lessons began and ended.

You (the teacher) should read the information that students need to write on student math logs. (See Example 8-4; pg.123) I read log information two to three times a week near the end of class periods. When students left school on Friday they had information for the current week. To write a math log follow these steps.

1) Staple six or seven line sheets of paper together.

2) Use dates to write weekly headings. (see page 64, weekly heading 10/11-10/15)

3) Draw a rectangle to set up a parental signature box. (A parent should sign a student's log weekly to verify reading of information)

4) The log should be dated in the left margin to show where information is written for each day, Monday through Friday.

5) Different colored pens, etc. should be used to highlight collected work and homework.

6) Use heavily shaded double lines to end each week.

Although students may not start student math logs on the first day of a school year, the teacher's log should be set up and written on the first day. When student logs are set up, student logs should be brought up to the current date by starting with information from the first day of school. Following is an example of first day of school information and a date to show where second day information will be written. Parents should have information for Monday through Friday of every week, especially when there are interruptions such as student assemblies, half days, etc. Some parents will question why a student was given only three assignments to complete during a week. A log clarifies missed assignments due to class *interruptions*.

8/29 | students completed attendance cards, assigned seats, started discussing classroom rules

8/30 | ______________________________________

Student logs should be collected at least twice during a semester. Two to three weeks of information should be randomly selected and checked. Each week checked should represent one daily assignment and be given credit based on correctness, completion of information and a parental signature. (my students make a good effort to get parental signatures)

Providing parents with weekly information resulted in a lower number of parents contacting me to ask what students did in the classroom. Students were accountable for writing logs and parents were accountable for reading them. This was one more strategy that *eased* my duties as a teacher. Students did not want to be embarrassed during parent-teacher conferences. They knew I had master logs to show parents. I usually used a log written by a student who did excellent work to show parents exactly how student logs should be written because my logs contained information not given to students to copy. (information such as where I left off for a lesson, etc.)

The log also gave absent students an opportunity to obtain missed work without interrupting class sessions. Absent students simply borrowed another student's log to copy missed assignments. Students transferring into the class after the start of the school year had the opportunity to obtain all work assigned during the semester. They were able to use the information to review missed work, seek tutoring, etc. Some parents of new students actually looked at my log and made the decision that their son or daughter had missed too much work to be successful in the class. They requested their child be assigned to another math class. If the request could not be accommodated, it was understood that they had a responsibility to seek tutoring, etc. to help the child be successful. I informed them I was willing to work with the student as long as the student displayed appropriate behavior in the classroom. There were also good students I could use to help meet the student's needs.

Writing a class activity log can prove to be motivational and fun for students. My students did quite a lot of work using colored pencils. They were able to be totally creative with the way they used colored to enhance the appearance of log information and class work. The information I read for students to copy had to be written in pencil or ink. Reading student logs was one of my most enjoyable experiences. The way students used color was outstanding. This was also apparent in much of the math work I received from students. The majority of students' work posted on bulletin boards was enhanced by using colored pencils.

As students continue their education log writing can prove to be a valuable experience. Many of my former students returned to inform me that they were able to organize and keep track of information for high school classes. Writing a class activity log in middle school clearly eased the transition they had to make into high school.

EXAMPLE 8-4

Class Activity Log (Math)

	10/11 to 10/15	Sig.
10/11	bellwork (checked), assigned pg.109;5-8 and 17-20, hmwk, pg. 109;25	
10/12	checked and discussed 10/11 assignment, 8th grade assembly	
10/13	bellwork (checked), test 4 given, started game preparation activity	
10/14	test 4 discussed and sent home, assigned pg.135;1-8 and 14-28;	
	hmwk; complete unfinished problems	
10/15	no class /half day /hours 4,5,6	
	10/18 to 10/22	Sig.
10/18	collected bellwork (10/11 and 10/13), assignment and hmwk. (10/11),	
	checked assignment 10/14, continued cooperative learning activity:pg. 201	
	(explore activity)	
10/19		

FINAL THOUGHTS

It's been thirty-three years since I started teaching in 1976. July 2009 was the beginning of my ninth school year of being officially retired from teaching. The years have passed quickly since I retired July 2001. I've worked on several projects that include writing this book. I've been busy but not too busy to stay in touch with former co-workers who continue doing their best to educate students.

I will take the manuscript for this book to a printer before December 2009. I've had to be patient with myself as I've tried to complete the book by a specific date that's changed every week for the last three months (This also happened when I wrote my classroom management book, When Kids Don't Listen).

I'm very fortunate to have several people, including school principals, who are waiting for a copy of the book. I continually get inquiries to conduct seminars or workshops and look forward to fulfilling requests after completing this book. I'm amazed at how the book has progressed. It started as a simple task of minor changes that resulted in a complete overhaul. I find it interesting that I've updated my classroom management book every eight years since the first book was written in 1994. I believe this will be the last classroom management book I write. I really want to devote more time to entertainment projects that I've started but have not completed. However, deep in my heart, I know I will never lose the desire to teach math or be a classroom management consultant.

I made a commitment in the early years of my teaching career to stand up for the rights of students to receive a quality education. I've paid a high price to make it happen because I sacrificed a substantial amount of guaranteed retirement income by retiring early to give myself the opportunity to extent my work as a classroom management consultant to other schools. I know for a fact that I would not have written my second classroom management book or this book had I continued to teach math until I could receive full retirement benefits. The second book was written after I retired and had time to really think about what I needed to write to update the first book.

I've had many interesting interactions as I've continued my work as a consultant. But I'm somewhat amazed that there are people who continue to ask the following question. *"What subjects is your book good for?"* I give the same answer. *"The subject doesn't matter. It's about student behavior."* I hope I've clarified with this book that reading, mathematics and other academic subjects are not more important than managing student behavior. But, I've decided that if it's easier to understand my point of view by expressing how I feel about classroom management as an academic subject, I CAN DO THAT!! How about, *"Student Behavior 101, Student Behavior 102, etc."* Sounds good to me!

Now, the final question that I need to answer is, do I agree with people who say, *THESE KIDS HAVE CHANGED!* Well, I concede that, yes, in general, they have. They want more, expect more, demand more, etc. etc. etc. Therefore, we who are in charge need to *get with the program* and give them more; *more love, more knowledge, more guidance on how to love themselves and love others, more guidance on how to become self-sufficient before growing up to become husbands, wives, parents, etc., etc., etc.*

To the extent that those of us in charge can make a difference, let's insure that the phrase *These Kids Have Changed* represent change that's good and productive. Let's insure that the changes that occur in our children will be a blessing to them, to their mothers, fathers, sisters, brothers and many others who can be blessed as a result of what they do. Let's insure that we do our part so that one day soon our nation will be able to say:

"YES! THESE KIDS HAVE CHANGED, AND THE WORLD IS A BETTER PLACE BECAUSE OF IT!!

I'm going to close now with the hope that I've written everything I wanted to write. I pray that this book contributes to continuing my work in classroom management as I find and encourage others to find *new ways to think about old strategies*. I'm so grateful for the success that I've had with my first two books. I pray that this book will be a blessing for parents, teachers, administrators, churches and other individuals and organizations that would dare to step up to the plate and do what it takes to resolve behavioral issues that prevent young people from obtaining the best education possible.

I have no regrets! I know that the work I've done in classroom management prior to writing this book has helped a multitude of administrators, teachers and students in several schools. The benefits will continue for generations to come. I AM BLESSED!!

SUPPLEMENT

{Supplemental materials can be duplicated.}

- **8½ in. x 11in. grid**
- **Checklist (teacher)**
- **Checklist (parent)**
- **Letter/Codes Sheet (with codes)**
- **Letter/Codes Sheet (without codes)**
- **Self-Monitoring Chart (with week days)**
- **Self-Monitoring Chart (without week days)**
- **Homework Chart (one person)**
- **Homework Chart (group chart)**
- **Documentation Sheet**
- **Students' Creed**

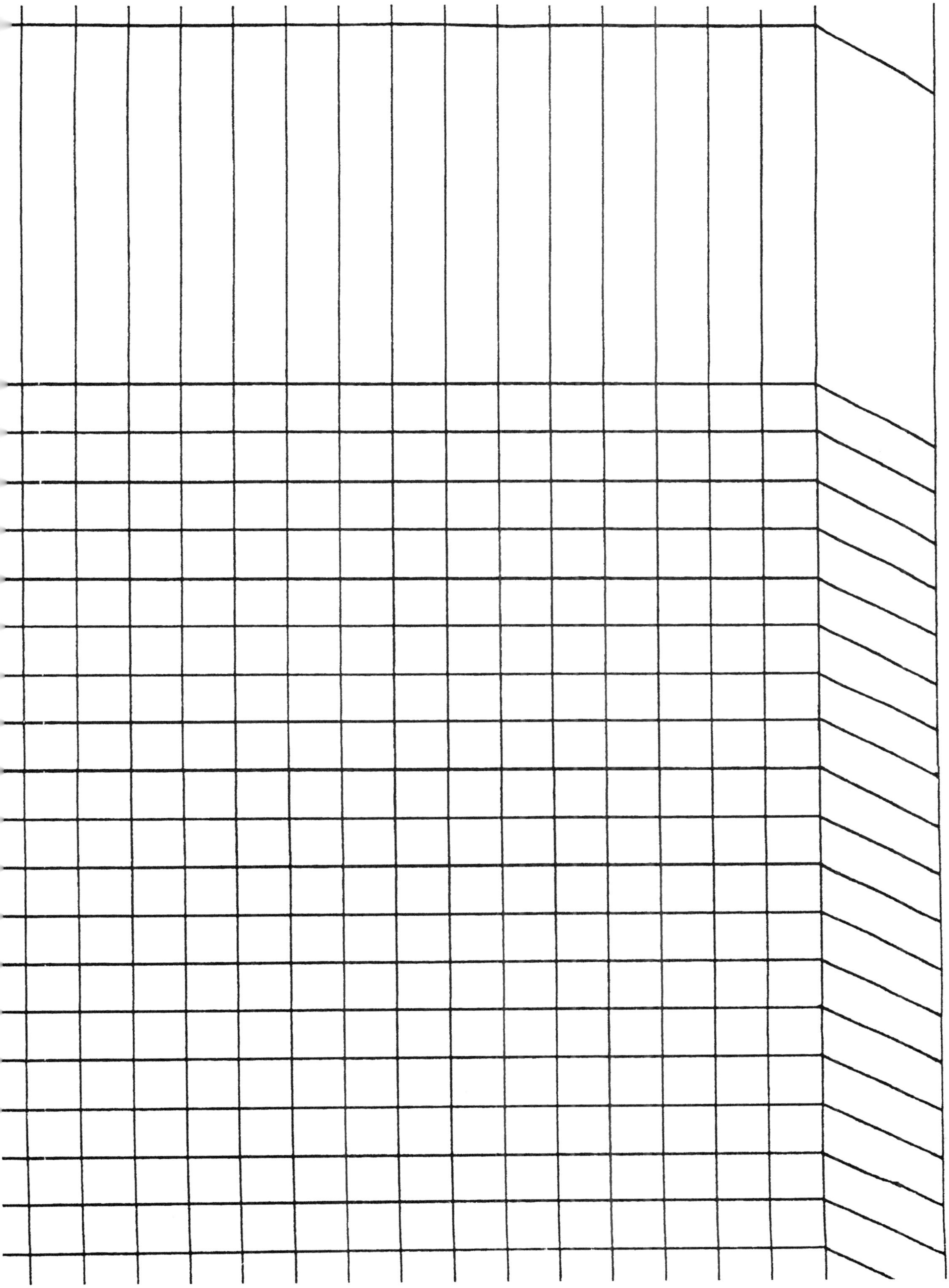

CLASSROOM MANAGEMENT CHECKLIST (teacher)

Classroom Appearance	Excellent	Good	Need Improvement
teacher's desk			
bulletin boards			
student desks, tables, etc.			
bookcases, shelves, etc.			
chalkboard			
floor			
door			
windows & surrounding area			
other:			

Discipline Plan	Yes	No	Need Improvement
written discipline plan implemented in the classroom			
written discipline plan effective in classroom			
written discipline plan implemented in the hall area (hall duty, escorting students, etc.)			
written discipline plan effective in hall area			
teacher appears relaxed			
teacher's talking level is good			
teacher comments are effective when responding to inappropriate student behavior (non-repetitive, etc.)			
discipline plan includes opportunities for students to see their behavior patterns in writing			
administrator/s provided with written copy of discipline plan upon request			

Student Behavior	Excellent	Good	Need Improvement
movement in classroom is good			
all student movement in the classroom is monitored by the teacher			
movement outside of classroom is good			
student movement in the hall area is monitored by the teacher			
objects on student desks, tables, etc. are approved and appropriate for lesson/s			
students' talking level is good			
students talk by permission only			
students follow teacher instructions			
students are engaged in lesson/s			
learning centers implemented			
cooperative learning activities implemented			

COMMENTS

CHECKLIST FOR PARENT/S (home monitoring)

Discipline Plan	Yes	No	Need Improvement
you've explained rules that you expect your child/children to follow			
your child/children consistently follow rules you've established			
you've given instructions on how your child/children should complete assigned tasks in the home			
you've verified that your child/children understand how to complete assigned tasks in the home			
your child/children consistently complete assigned tasks in the home			
you are relaxed when interacting with your child/children who display disrespectful behavior			
your talking level is good when interacting with your child/children who display disrespectful behavior			
your comments are effective when responding to disrespectful behavior displayed by your child/children (non-repetitive)			
you are willing to work with your child's/children's teachers to implement and/or reinforce student behavioral expectations in school			

LETTER / CODES SHEET

Date: ______________________
Teacher: ______________________
Subject / Hour: ______________________

Student, ______________________, must complete writing assignment number/s ______________ as a result of inappropriate behavior. (see below)

Due Date: ______________________
Number of times: ______________________
Parental signature: ______________________

Writing Assignment

1. **Respect for staff persons**: Students must respect administrators, teachers and all staff persons. (custodians, lunchroom workers, etc.) Students must answer questions asked by a staff person.
2. **Respect for other students**: Students are responsible for avoiding behavior that is detrimental to the achievement of educational goals for all students. Students must refrain from destroying the property of others, name calling, verbal or physical threats, etc.

Behavior Codes

B-behavior
Bl-blatant
C-chewing
D-disruptive
Di-distracting
E-entrance
Ex-exit
F-fighting
H-hitting
I-insubordination
L-laughing
N-noise
O-out of seat
P-playing
R-running
____

S-standing
Sh-shoving
Sl-sleeping
T-talking
W-walking
AO-accepting an object
PO-passing an object
AS-attempting to sleep
FD-foot on back of desk
OF-objects on floor
NA-not paying attention
SO-sliding object on floor
TH-throwing an object
UI-unprepared for instruction
WT-wasting time
____

M1-missing pen or pencil
M2-missing paper
M3-missing textbook
D1-wearing a coat
D2-wearing a jacket
D3-wearing a hat
C1-carrying food
C2-carrying a beverage
____
____
____
____
____
____
____
____

____
____
____

Student's behavior pattern (transferred from Discipline Chart): ______________

____

Other Comments.

LETTER / CODES SHEET

Date: ______________________________

Teacher: ______________________________

Subject / Hour: ______________________________

Student, ______________________________, must complete writing assignment number/s ______________ as a result of inappropriate behavior. (see below)

Due Date: ______________________________

Number of times: ______________________________

Parental signature: ______________________________

Writing Assignment

1. **Respect for staff persons**: Students must respect administrators, teachers and all staff persons. (custodians, lunchroom workers, etc.) Students must answer questions asked by a staff person.
2. **Respect for other students**: Students are responsible for avoiding behavior that is detrimental to the achievement of educational goals for all students. Students must refrain from destroying the property of others, name calling, verbal or physical threats, etc.

Behavior Codes

Student's behavior pattern (transferred from Discipline Chart): ______________________

Other Comments.

Homework Chart: ______________________
(name)

SUBJECT/S						Homework Completion Codes						Homework Completion Codes						Homework Completion Codes						Homework Completion Codes

Homework Completion Codes: **E**-Excellent **G**-Good **F**-Fair **N**-Need Improvement

Homework Chart: ______________________

Names						Homework Completion Codes						Homework Completion Codes						Homework Completion Codes

Homework Completion Codes: **E**-Excellent **G**-Good **F**-Fair **N**-Need Improvement

Self-Monitoring Chart: ______________________________

Assignment: ______________________________

Assigned By: ______________________________

Progress Codes: **E**-Excellent **G**-Good **I**-Improved **P**-Poor

	Weekly Progress Code =							**Weekly Progress Code =**						
	Mon	Tues	Wed	Thurs	Fri	Sat	Sun	Mon	Tues	Wed	Thurs	Fri	Sat	Sun

Self-Monitoring Chart: ______________________________

Assignment: ______________________________

Assigned By: ______________________________

Progress Codes: **E**-Excellent **G**-Good **I**-Improved **P**-Poor

	Weekly Progress Code =							**Weekly Progress Code =**						

STUDENT'S NAME/GRADE

DOCUMENTATION SHEET

STAFF PERSON	DATE:HOUR	BEHAVIOR	ACTION TAKEN	see other side(✓)

Students' Creed

I'm an intelligent human being.
I will assume responsibility for my behavior.
When I make the decision to behave I'm proud of myself.
If I misbehave I will accept consequences for my behavior.

I'm an intelligent human being.
I will not display inappropriate behavior in school.

I'm an intelligent human being.
I will respect the right of other students to be educated.

I'm an intelligent human being.
I will respect all administrators, teachers and other staff persons.

I'm an intelligent human being.
I will do my best to report to my classes and assigned locations on time.

I'm an intelligent human being.
I will enter all classes with required supplies.

I'm an intelligent human being.
I will not enter any classroom with unapproved clothing, food or other items.

I'm an intelligent human being.
I will respect the educational process
every school day
of every week
and every year
until I complete my studies.

......I Am An Intelligent Human Being......